Flowers of Bitumen

Little Parisian Poems

Émile Goudeau

Translated By Richard Robinson

Sunny Lou Publishing Company
Portland, Oregon, USA
http://www.sunnyloupublishing.com

1st Edition, Revised & Corrected: June 19, 2022
Original Publication Date: January 19, 2021

Translation Copyright © 2021 Richard Robinson.
All rights reserved.

ISBN: 978-1-7354776-6-4

* * *

This translation from the French of *Fleurs du Bitume* is based on the first edition from 1885 by publisher Paul Ollendorff. (The first publication of *Fleurs du Bitume* was in 1878 by publisher Alphonse Lemerre.)

Contents

DEDICATION (1885) 7
THE ROMANS 9
   The Asphalt Fairy 9
   The Enfranchised 11

CHAVIRETTE 17
   Chavirette 17

A CULLING ON ASPHALT 21
   Inscription 21
   Memory Lane 21
   Watching the Stars 22
   Song of Brutal Love 22
   Solo Aubade 23
   Matins 24
   To Your Green Eyes 25
   To Her Who Has Green Eyes 26
   P.P.C. 27
   Let's be Slaves! 27
   To One Who Despises Women 28
   Why I Don't Marry You 30
   The Last Waltz 32
   To the Woman with Blue Eyes 32
   Sonnet 33
   Sonnet 34
   Sonnet 34
   The Other Side of the Model 35
   The Fall 37

   Song for Nini 37
   The Beauty and the Beast 38
   Artistic Revenge 40
   Last Day 42
   Same Old Song 43
   Scattered Music 45
   Lost Words 46
   Redivivus 47
   Alone! 48
   Sonnet 50

THE GREEKS 53
   Queen of Spades 53
   The Greeks 55

A SEASON OF SPLEEN 59
   I Would Like to Live in the Woods 59
   Round of Remorse 60
   The Long March 62
   Desperando 63
   Misery's Gibbet 64
   Imprecation 65
   Toward the Tombs 66
   Mortal Triangle 67
   ? 67
   Dilemma 68
   True Triplets of Misery 68
   Voices Carried by the Wind 70
   Hope! 72
   Promenade 73
   Awakening 74

In the Old Fashioned Way	75
On the Way to Charenton	76
Don Quixote	77
Being in Paris	78
Bitch of Poverty	79

HISSED!! 83
    Renown 83
    Hissed!! 85

DEDICATION (1885)

To her who turns pale
When passion possesses her heart,
As the throng by a conqueror's foot,
I lend my male force.

Now, when the triumphal crowd,
Street entertainer, and bookmaker
Abstain from mocking laughter:
Hercules takes off for Omphale;

And, despite his vigorous biceps,
Samson lets his hair drop
Under his companion's scissors.

Delilah: for a single kiss,
I quite allow you to raze
My four hundred Spanish chateaus.

        – Émile GOUDEAU.

THE ROMANS

The Asphalt Fairy

TO THE POET

The train, which brought you from distant provinces,
    Is long since departed again.
Forget, child, your lame little naïveties,
    Grow up, you who were petite.
Paris, which is mine, is a vast arena
    For love and ambition;
The street today is the only sovereign:
    Bring it your devotion.

You have no home in this great city?
    Visit the inns of luck!
Contraband friends and fucks...
    All can be found at the bazaar.
Others, like you, but more Bohemian,
    Have risen from the sidewalk
To make, of their strange lives, poems
    Pompously clothed in hope.

Also, stop thinking of forests and prairies...
    The squares are better raked!
Over there, suns cradled reveries:
    Here, gaslights have replaced them...
What do you care about the rose, the humble daisy,
    And the insufferable muguet?
The bitumen has flowers whose perfume arouses:
    Go then: grab me a bouquet.

THE POET

I'm going; I close the book
Where I inscribed my virtues;
My remorses are overcome
By my desire to see life.

Also, I give the sack
To Plutarch's dead men.
Into the crowd I embark,
Fearless and unprejudiced.

I will go among the fog,
Under flourishing gas lamps
If it's certain that in Paris
All sprouts from the bitumen.

If the song of a twenty-year-old
And his stoked stanzas
Run there like fairies
Through the rain and fine weather;

If ancient Poetry,
Quitting the sacred valley,
Comes to Apollo to pray there,
To pay him in ambrosia;

If, indeed, near the gutters,
The noctambulant poet
Can hear, at daybreak,
The warbling of birds;

Or if – superb novelty! –
The dream, having left the heart,
Can sing a vanquishing song there,
Without grass, nest, or water.

The Enfranchised

I

Do you see them pass, the enfranchised beauties?
On the sand-strewn paths and blanched routes,
That the slave waterer humectates with long jets of water,
Their eight-leaf-spring chariots fly, and the Lutecian[1]
Onlooker cries out: "Oh! The beautiful heathen!"

They pass at a trot along the Elysian way,
Leaving behind them the old palace of kings;
And to the covered forum where so many laws were passed,
They climb, making Parthian oglings,
Until the Triumphal Arc of Bonaparte Caesar.
O Romans of Paris, look at them from a distance
As they pass in their pride, ebony whip in fist:

As if, at those beautiful charioteers' call,
The quadrigae came down from the old bas-reliefs
That an Ausonian sculptor had sculpted in marble;
That's how they go to the Bois de Bologne
To take in the spring. The wide, Maillotine gate,
Spreads wide before their libertine throng.
Soon along the paths, under a big golden sun,
They are soliciting Johns around the great lake.

Sometimes, crossing their chariot, a pubescent equestrian
Salutes them amicably with his right hand;
While a senator, a consul, or an old tribune,
Devours them stealthily with his eyes.
Oh! Venus has given charm to her priestesses!
In their hair, one smells the breeze of caresses
That stir the wide folds of their trailing veils;
Their eyes are enlarged by Kold-Indian;[2]

---

[1] Lutecian: an inhabitant of Lutèce, the ancient Roman name for the city of Paris.

[2] Kold-Indian: presumably a drug (like digitalis) or beauty aid. See also "Make-up" in Théadore Hannon's *Rimes de joie* for sundry suchlike.

Like a rival pair of vermillion auroras,
Two pearls from Ashur gleam in their ears;
Under the embroidered peplos those love warrioresses
Have locked away their candid bosom; and it is to
Cover their flanks that, with aching hands,
The Sère de Lyon have woven silks,
And the Celto-Belgians produced linen.
Look at them pass in their divine luxury!

My Hercules! but they used to be slaves!
Walnut sabots served as their fetters,
And, in tough canvas blouses, their Sirenian
Charms were something else altogether.
They were seen, over the Gallian plains,
Holding a willow branch between long fingers,
Pasturing along ditches, or leading to water,
Either the ovine family or the porcine race.
Clymene, whom a prince of the blood was
Mad about, in bygone days, served a matron:
A culinary vestal, with blue eyes,
She tended the fire at the far end of a greasy dugout;
Cynthia, with a face like Minerva's,
A mere child then, poor pretty serf, went
To sew Syrian fabrics with her needle,
Which she buys today for next to nothing;
Araminte, a brunette, and Lesbia, a blond,
Used to bring Mr. Everyman his linen:
Fateful times! when Chloé, Cupidon's flunkey,
For her father, Cerbère, manned the bell-pull.

But all of them, as they chase an importunate beast,
Have forgotten the years of bad luck,
And drink pleasure eagerly as if there were no tomorrow.
Shame on the awful slavery of virtue,
That dungeon of duty, that deadbolt for virgins!
On Vesta's altar, let's let the candles smoke
And burn out; Evohé! with a prodigious leap
They mount fortune's wheel, towards heaven,
Glittering with riches and with life,

THE ROMANS

Where the thirst to enjoy themselves is finally satisfied.
Goodbye poverty! Happy days, here we come!
Minerva is a sot, evohé for Venus!
No more brown bread, spoilt milk, rancid butter!
Modesty is a shackle! Shamelessness a freedom!

Nowadays, you cannot pursue them, O Remorse!
To help them flee are their eight-leaf-spring chariots
With their fiery steeds from Great Britain!
Renown accompanies them with its trumpet,
For they have made the most faraway pretors bow,
As well as patricians, and absolute dictators,
And even the princes of old monarchies...

Do you see them pass, the enfranchised beauties?

II

DONUM CŒLESTE, COLUMBÆ![3]

One day, thinking quietly on my dear profaner,
As I wandered silently along the Séquane,
A naïve and very old spectacle caught my eye:
Three plebeians, leaning against the parapet,
And two Gaulish warriors, rutilant under their braccae
Dyed the color of wounds by the murmex,[4]
Were looking at a fisherman looking at the water.
Suddenly, I heard a very confused and noisy
Chirping of birds over the sound of the swell
That the queen of the world eternally moves.
Where did that strange concert come from? – On the sill
Of a boutique, near a porch swollen with pride,
A thousand birds cackled in painted cages;
A merchant, with gloomy eyes, faded lips,
And black hooked nails, was selling his prisoners.

---

[3]*donum... columbae*: Latin for "doves, the gift of heaven."

[4]Murmex: literally, "ant." Possibly a reference to the Myrmidons of Thessaly.

Now, as in my pocket jangled some *deniers*,
A surprisingly pagan thought seized me
And I stepped into that plebeian's shop.
Seeing me, the birds began to prattle:
Puit! Puit! Puit! they said, as if begging me to
O, i, o, take us, *la, ut, la*, from our cells!
But, ignoring them, I purchased two doves,
Albes,[5] the both of them, with amorous eyes,
And suited for consecration to the gods.
I was crazy at that time for the cult of Aphrodite,
The naked, loved, and cursed white deity.
The cult had a joyous and mad nest, a temple,
Located on Haussmann Way, twenty steps above the street:
There lived, under the obscure calm of sanctuary,
In the costume and posture of rituary,
My Lesbia, busy at losing her Latin
While reading her fate in a deck of cards.
O sweet dream, o Lesbia, o erstwhile virgin!
In the atrium an old cocky concierge slave
Casts a vague, indulgent smile at
The doves; but, billing and cooing or dreaming,
The three of us pass in our classical pride;
And, serious, I mounted, over a Persian rug,
Silent and slow, the twenty steps, and then
I pressed the brass bell at the door.
A rather ugly slave opened, and once her cold
Pupils had recognized my solemn face,
I was soon allowed to tread the parvis of that sacred place,
Where a faint, nearly spent perfume hung in the air.
On the sacred hearth where logs from a tree
Writhed in flames, a marble Venus stood,
Magnificent and proud between two large, chiseled torches,
Lifting her chin and gazing at exiled Olympians;
All naked and armless she was; but one could guess
The Victorious One has better means to defend herself;
And raising the two doves above my head
I said: "By dreams that are disillusioned,
And illusions that are dead for distress,

---

[5]*Albes*: presumably "white" (from Latin, *albus, alba, album*).

THE ROMANS

Greetings to you, Venus! greetings to you, priestess!
Greetings! having traveled a long way, this pilgrim
Never weary of your cult, unbridled Aphrodite,
I come to consecrate to you these two white doves,
You who have never drunk the blood of hecatombs,
So that, from the first rays of dawn, their voices
Might coo for you a song both sweet and rude!"
Having said this, I released the birds who flew
To Lesbia's breast, where my vows followed them,
But she, practiced in the rites, kissed them
On their cajoling beaks made drunk by her lips.
Then, to fete the love that Bacchus accompanies,
We drank Falerne[6] from Champagne[7]
And ate truffles; and, on that sacramental evening,
Having executed the mystery and shadow, on the altar
We offered to Venus a passionate litany,
Which sobs of infinite fervor lent their rhythm to.

At dawn, I escaped that temple of love,
While swearing, to the god of Styx, a prompt return;
But my Muse having summoned me to recite
Austere songs to the skillful tune of a lyre,
I broke my word, and, negligent devotee,
I wandered till month's end, far from your eyes,
O my Lesbia! – One evening I received tablets
Exhaling a faint scent of violets.
The priestess wrote to her priest: "Incredible man,
If you don't want me to hate you forever,
Come dine with me on Haussmann Way, and bring
Two tickets for the circus (*Panem et circenses*:
Real Romans always go see gladiators
And naked athletes with their seductive torsos)."
I had to obey, I obeyed! – Victims
Never suspicious when they are being led into a trap!
Lesbia, welcoming me on the sill, smiled at me
In a bizarre and false fashion; my mind,

---

[6]Falerne: a highly-reputed wine in antiquity, from Falerno, in Campania, Italy.

[7]Champagne: a region (in France).

Doubtless obliterated by the scents in the temple,
Could guess at nothing; and it was with an ample
And noble step that I entered. From atop the pedestal
Venus cast a cold, metallic glance at me
With an incredible, menacing, enigmatic look on her face;
But I understood nothing. I sat down at my place,
And, under great, bright, flickering flames,
Dishes of vaguely-sculpted food were offered to me
That I ate, without knowing what they were: my mouth,
Ten times more than flesh, loves crimson wine,
And a hundred times more than wine, loves kisses.
Now, Lesbia was beautiful, and with bold fingers
I wanted to unlace and open her tunic;
But Lesbia burst out into sardonic laughter, –
A crazy laugh, that pealed, vibrated, resonated;
Then, seeing my face grow pale, she stopped
And said: "Look at those pieces! Our bellies are the tombs
Of the two celestial gifts made to Venus." The doves!
I had eaten the two divine birds! What horror!
Hey! The idol's eyes were burning with a fury,
Her missing arms seemed to rise up in rage.
I got up from my place, turning like a wolf in a cage:
"Forgive me!" I cried. And Venus replied: "No!"
                                                    – Me!
The last surviving son of the *Peuple-Roi*,[8]
The last partisan of antique Paganism,
The sole worshipper of immodest Venus,
The unique specimen of regretted past,
Me, priest of Aphrodite! – O detested *fatum*!
Me who has never drunk the blood of a hecatomb, –
I had eaten the birds of Venus, the doves!!
Lesbia, herself, laughed like a madwoman. Forever,
Priestess of Pluto, more than a priestess of love,
May you, who made me commit such infamy, be cursed!

And ever since that time I've suffered Aphrodite's hatred.

---

[8]*Peuple-Roi*: literally the "People-King," It seems to be a reference to a government ruled by the people, such as the early Roman Republic.

CHAVIRETTE

Chavirette

Chavirette's come home again: she's tired. – After all,
When drifts of fog give you the catarrh
One can easily get disgusted now and then
For that long hard slog on the bitumen. –
She's a *fille de joie:*[9] she goes and she comes
On a sidewalk; beat cops find her to their taste;
She says: "Howdy blondie!..." or "Hey handsome!..."
She takes to anyone; she sticks to you like paste.

She's come home. She wants to dream alone, –
On what? on nothing: spleen, vague disgust.
Those whom fate, under its grindstone, crush,
Have unconscious bouts of instinct, the gestures
Of castaways while the gulf enshrouds them.

Now, the women one sees inured to real evils
Possess an immense fund in their fearful souls:
Stores of stupid and sickly sentimentality; woes
Betide them; and when their heart is full, it overflows.

All alone, she starts to cry, Chavirette.
Why? no reason: her days are all the same;
And, above her head, in the black frame,
Her portrait smiles still, that same terrible grin,
Caught between two obscenely feverous scenes.

Poor fallen angels! poor vile beings!
Poor profaned bodies one dares not call women!
Guitars of love really, not violins,
Whose soul, whose body, whose entire being is prey

---

[9]*fille de joie*: prostitute or woman of pleasure; literally "girl of joy."

To the first man to come along and say: I want to pay.
You're the one the passersby call *fille de joie*.

Joy! oh! that old patrician word is roaring
With such a dirty, democratic whoring.
To hang such a sign in front of like boutique!
Does one say joy instead of: Here lies?
Joy? To appease the ardor of each Sodomite!
Joy? To quench the thirst of every soak!
At that uncouth hour when drunkards low,
What joy is that, being men's feeding trough?

Say: are you mindful sometimes of bygone days,
When you wore your chastity like a perfume,
And had a blanched soul in a suntanned body?
Do you not see still, in that childhood room,
A maternal phantom leaning over your bed,
Grazing your forehead with her loving kiss?
Are you mindful still how, when Sunday rolled around,
Nose to the wind, hands on your hips,
You ran circles on the lawn, in the Church playground?

Ah! enough! They're old already, like an old moon
Those circles, those kisses! a mother! oh! ouch!
Like an importunate hand that looms,
Like an accursed storm that slaps and clouts.

Think on a time when your heart began to stir.
At sixteen, what the hell, one falls in love!
A young man neared a corner of the hearth, in winter,
And held out his hand to you, he courted you.
But you scorned that village cock:
At thirteenth in line he was last, like the drummer,
And, although he told you to wait till he came back,
He will not come back; – you even less, I wager.

So be it! – You came to Paris; in a garret,
A sewing machine, acquired at so much per month,
Barely paid the concierge's rent,

And the meager meals of a virgin laborer:
It was then that the devil asserted his rights.
Say, do you remember love's spring, or
That young man who waited for you for so long?
Ah! distant memory: same heart, same glass,
And to cap it all, same age: eighteen!

– To love just one person in life, is that a crime?

But after him, how many others? The pits
Opened up beneath your feet, insouciant marchers,
And you stumbled, like a sublime angel
Who would launch itself from heaven to gain hell.
Remorse was scattered to the wind of passing fancies,
Folly, wild dancing, shook its little bells,
And you heard no more than the high-pitched scales
Of laughter, that proved fatal precursors to sobs.

Now, it's over! Cry! Your soul is dead,
And your body is soiled like a slobbered rag;
You're missing teeth, your breath is bad,
You have too much rouge and too little hair;
You were a mistress once, now you are a slave,
The slave of abject and repulsive desires;
In the street, at midnight, you hail passersby,
The first man to come along, you dry his slaver!

How old are you now? Not yet twenty-six!

Ah, well! no, it's not for that she weeps.
Not her childhood, not her fiancé, not her lover,
Nor the shame of nipping an entire life in the bud,
Which causes no nightmares, or torments, or trouble.
That girl has no longer a head or a heart,
No heart to sense the depth of evil,
No mind to laugh about it: she is dumb with grief;
All is dead inside her, except the animal.

Like a very old, tired, deaf, and vile ass

Remembers blows received with certain fondness,
Like a felled tree under the blows of an ax
That seems to bleed and whose branches cry out,
She has morose sentiments and instincts,
And the lamentation of everything that dies;
Her tears are like a plaint of things.

Maybe I pity you, but also I hate you,
O Ninon of the sidewalk,[10] o venenous Phyrne![11]
You largely return the evil that's been done to you:
Your kisses are unwholesome, your soul is hateful.
To speak with you with some amity, one must
Be older and younger than a patriarch.
Evil never does things halfway:
If that filth you call a body stirs a little,
Disgust fills the heart and chases pity away.

Pardon me, friends, for telling so stupid a story
And one that descends into such gibberish;
But I had known her in her heyday,
And loved her still, vaguely, in my memory...
It's horrible, today, to see how far she's fallen!

---

[10]Ninon...: probably a reference to Ninon de l'Enclos, 1620-1705, a courtesan, woman of letters, and woman of wit.

[11]Phyrne: a Greek courtesan of the 4th century BC.

A CULLING ON ASPHALT

Inscription

One sees nothing but hope, illusion, love.
Hope diminishes with each step and rushes off;
Illusion exfoliates and falls without returning;
As for love, it's an ancient bit of humbug:
From the banal glass of gross gaiety,
One tastes nothing but adulterated love anymore...
The old wines are gone, the low-quality ones console you,
      O poor, poor humanity!

Memory Lane

O lane, there you are adorned with faded flowers
That give off vague, faint scents;
Nests, deserted years ago since your departure,
Sleep buried in the emptiness of hedges.

The hills in the distance rise, crowned
By rolling fog, and lengthen in their folds;
Enveloped by ivy, some ruins are found,
And, under my feet, fields that mourning takes hold of.

Autumn landscape, where silence reigns,
Where, in the blue mist, the dream is cradled:
Those are the bygone days I want to live again!

I don't know if time, that prismatic painter,
Knows how to render the distant years more poetically,
But I still miss you, memory lane!

Watching the Stars

From the end of a mirliton[12]

Autumn night, at my window,
I was breathing in the scant rural air
That God distributes in Paris,
And watching the shooting stars
Pass, slow or swift,
Across surprised zodiacs.

Clearly the houris amuse themselves
Seeing if their diamonds can be used
To line the face of heaven;
There they trace, those gossips,
The ephemeral arabesques
Of our capricious loves.

Under the canopy of an immobile bed,
Passion lights up and dies down
To vanish finally without a trace.
But when, in a sky less prolix,
Will I find a fixed star,
A fixed star of love?

Song of Brutal Love

When the last fabric of fine embroidery
Falls from your shoulder, and uncovers your breasts,
When it drops reluctantly to your well-nourished hips
And pauses as it veils the curvature of your back,
When you let the *batiste* drop to your feet,
Without lifting a finger, without breathing a word,
One might think he saw appear the dream of an *artiste*
In the pale, veined flesh of your flawless marble.

---

[12]mirliton: a reed flute.

Marble made flesh, and now you're a woman again;
With a coquettish air, putting up your hair,
You kindle the flame in me by your regard
And throw every bit of yourself into my nervous arms.
I hold you: let me plant burning kisses,
Strong as wine, on your neck, on your lips...
Let me indulge in the mad passion of amorous fevers;
Let me get drunk on that divine contact.

Ah!... my heart throbs, my mouth is parched;
Around me, everything disappears; no, nothing exists
But the rouge that blushes on your empurpled cheek,
And the lascivious quivers of your naked breasts!
Nothing! nothing, except the words your mouth murmurs
When pleasure gleams in your half-shut eyes,
When I see your blond hair undulate,
And your heart swoon with joyous sobs!

Again! I want to see you again! What do I care
For my former friends, for my dreams of yesterday?
I have barely closed your door behind me,
And taken one hundred steps, ten steps on the path, –
O Mia, I want to rush back to your mouth,
To extract that sweet poison of love and pleasure!
Alone with that memory, far from you, on my bed,
I writhe in the despicable anguish of desire.

Solo Aubade

When I lay me down in the narrow coffin,
Mia! I will not think on or recall any longer
The days of my youth when I went like a king,
Telling, not counting, the beads of hope and strength,
Turning my life into a ring for your finger.

Mia! Under the funeral boards, I will miss
The sight of you, beloved and gleaming, at the back

Of bitter solitudes and bitter darknesses;
But I will have – which makes me shudder,
Just to think about them, hideous helminths.
I will no longer have your eyes, o Mia! for the sun,
I will no longer have your voice for celestial music,
I will no longer have your bright shiny laughter,
I will no longer have your ardent breast, nor all the rest,
And I will settle down to sleep with no hope of waking.

Given that I feel full of life then this morning,
Do not protest too much, princess of the spring,
If, when letting myself be guided where love leads me,
From your half-open mouth to your dazzling breasts,
My unquenched lips hasten to awaken you.

Matins

Midday! Midday! Midday! Midday!
Is it a Sunday? Is it a Monday?
A Tuesday? Or a Wednesday?
Thursday? Friday? Saturday?
I don't know: Midday! Midday!

In your arms the tender night,
Unappeasable Messaline,
Must not end at all.
Twelve times I curse the clock,
Whose brusque voice upends me,
And tells me twelve times: get up!

Basta! the Persian blinds are shut,
And the opaque pink curtains
Prolong the night at day;
Be my accomplice in error...
Again on your smooth breast,
Again a long-lasting kiss of love!

Those who love not, dark adepts
Of a ton of inept jobs,
Prefer the light of day.
What do I care, my sleeping beauty?
For us two lovers, a nightlight
Is worth a hundred times the sun.

But the city's tumultuousness,
In an uncivil way
Sneaks into our temple.
Another kiss on your mouth.
Look! Brutal reality
Sweeps away our dreams of night.

Sunday?... Thursday?... Saturday?
I don't know: it's already midday!

To Your Green Eyes

You are, my love, like a steep and lofty citadel,
Where the guards of the garrison never sleep:
The place has fabulous moats around it...
To cross and conquer it, one needs a bridge... of gold.

You are, my love, the gorgeous mystical fish,
That comes, goes, draws near, then escapes from the shore,
Flashing its blond scales in the aquatic mirror...
To catch it, o fisherman, one needs a net... of gold.

You are, my love, the blue bird that soars
Tracing misleading zigzags in its flight
On the star-filled, azure firmament of my dreams...
To reach it, o hunter, one needs an arrow... of gold.

You are, my love, just like the stoat
That lets nothing stain its precious white coat
That flees in horror from all that contaminate it,

Unless it's a question of sullying it... with gold.

But my love is pretty! and God knows if his pearls
Do well on her white neck, charm of the *flirtador*.[13]
The dove at nighttime lets blackbirds whistle!
She awaits the prodigal, and slays the calf... of gold.

To Her Who Has Green Eyes

Poor child with the hard heart, and hopeless dreams,
Whom gold has fashioned like a monstrance:
Empty! You were created, on a day of anger,
With elements that nothing warm sheds light on,
With the cold night and the cold ocean,
To appear just like a work of emptiness.
No! you no longer exist! What is a beam of moonlight
That passes and goes out without a trace
Found in the face of frightened mortals,
On whom the shadow suspends its long sacred veils?
Pale evocation that wanders under the leaves,
A phantom opening its bizarre emerald eyes
Full of feline regards! Dead to the bold
Who dare look you square in the face!
Dead to me! Evermore a phantom, idol! idol!
All alone I will flee without asking for an offering
Of happiness that Hell to all its children owes,
Far from adulators, and far from the triumphant,
Having laid a bitter irony on my heart,
Like a winding sheet on a chimerical cadaver,
Until the day when, weary of hateful exile,
I forget the lively absinthe of your eyes.

---

[13]*flirtador*: presumably flirt, from the Spanish, "flirteador."

P.P.C.

Oh! why, looking away,
Maintain a hostile lip
To the hive of joyous lovers
Who want to steal a kiss?

We have not, o my dear love,
      But a single day
To enjoy the blessed manna;
And well do you know your twenty years
      Won't last forever,
And after that the party's over.

And still you refuse me,
And you strike me with frail hands;
My kisses are kept in a cage:
You have clipped their wings.

I wanted to kneel
      Before you
And swear immortal love!
But, alas! your offended air
      Froze me...
Another will be less cruel.

Let's be Slaves!

Oh! if you should lose, sweetie! sweetie!
The secret charm that attracts me to you,
All that seduces, all that radiates,
Talisman of energetic and sweet love...
If you should lose it, sweetie! sweetie!

If the sky was to complain to the good God
That all his light had been taken
And placed behind your blue eyes

Making the first dawn pale in comparison!...
If the sky was to complain to the good God!

If you had no more strength or power,
To hold my life in your hands,
To bend to the yoke of obedience
My fanciful heart, rebellious to laws,
If you had no more strength or power.

If you should grant me my liberty...
I would join the vulgar ranks of men
Who no longer love anything: nor dream, nor beauty;
And life, alas! would hardly please me,
If you should grant me my liberty.

To One Who Despises Women

That poet, to tell the truth, is madly in love!
He moans!... A tremendous sob is heard
      Coming from the strings of his lute.
He found, he said, thousands of statues
That died frigidly under his hot kisses.
      O heart of woman, unpolished marble!

He went everywhere: in Seine,[14] in Seine-et-Oise:
He knew the Venus of city and village,
      The Venus of mountains and woods.
It's his study; it's his flora and his fauna;
Mind-withering science, he has turned jaundiced
      Studying their laws.

He weeps!... His unhappiness is moving, when one thinks about it.
Women!... made of absurdity and deceit;
      Of bronze: no heart, no brain.
O pitiless monsters! octopuses! ghouls! lemurs!
Oceans of tears, and downpours of insults

---

[14]Seine: a former department of France (from 1790 to 1967).

From cover to cover in-octavo.

When will he finish that hypocritical posture,
He who belies one hundred times his scribbled revery
    By real actions?
Alas, he does not want to fall into vulgarity;
A Don Quixote of the Ideal, he leaves for war
    Against his own passions.

My friend, if you want several instants of fever,
Ask your mistress for a kiss on the lips,
    Ephemeral oblivion of cares;
Let her do all the talking, without saying a word;
And, without her understanding, offer her your obole
    Of eulogistic alexandrines.

If by chance you want a more complete love,
Do not come to Lais's[15] place, o gloomy killjoy,
    To sing a *Requiem* over dessert.
Go, follow your young fiancée to the holy temple,
She whose pale memory dies in your thought,
    Like a flower in the desert.

But no, that alchemist has ironic tastes:
He seeks to combine Platonic souls
    With electrified nerves.
Café! tobacco! hashish! bedazzled ecstasies!
O Venus! Offer then extraordinary things
    To those poor blasé beings!

One begins to lie in wait for enormous deceits:
Blue suns! Green men! Welcome, deformed monsters!
    Hurray for eccentricity!
Then one polishes sonorous verses, one favors
The fake over the true word. What does nature
    And banal humanity matter?

Curses! if you speak the truth in your morose rhymes,

---

[15] Lais: a reference to Lais of Corinth, a famous Greek courtesan or *hetaira*.

If all is ugly: sky, men, and things, –
    If your bitter laughter is not false,
And if a mad and pure love no longer exists...
We must resign ourselves to sleeping without complaint
    The sleep of Schopenhauer.

Why I Don't Marry You

Brunettes! And how many blonds or brown-haired women!
With blue or black eyes! Young girls, distant
Already, whom I will never see again!
Very chaste flowers of nubile love whom I loved!
What a normal and flat road my life would have taken
Bound forever to your life!
Marriage! a terrible word! And yet
That word made me dream sometimes, watching
Some of those delicate profiles, without makeup,
In the calm of life seated at the corner of a hearth.
They had names, those who stayed with me,
And I was never able to see them again without emotion:
Jeanne, Albertine, Blanche, Elodie, Anne, and Rose,
With a bunch of sweet, sentimental nicknames.

Jeanne above all, with her profile of a Judeo-pagan
Framed by the blond hair of a Venetian,
So charming and derisive like a pretty blackbird.
I remember one evening when I called her "gem"
At the end of a very galant and idiotic acrostic...
The end of that sketch of a poem remains blank.

And why didn't I marry those Arabelles?
To be cuckolded later is no skin off my back, o beauties!
But to begin with I was weary and completely dumbfounded
By the efforts it would take to get merely to a "yes."
My laziness!... Think on it, vanished spouses,
That I have too little time, and Paris too many streets.

A CULLING ON ASPHALT

Come, go, hurry! Hurry, go, come!
The fiacre! the tramway! Not eating, not sleeping!
To visit the deputy mayor, at city hall,
That he might fix the day, the hour, when we might marry,
And to rectify, after much babble,
The blunders of a very uncivil, civil marriage;
Presto at the curate's, ditto the vicar's,
To pay for a not-too-very-long, but vulgar sermon,
And to wash my soul in the corner stoup.
And then there be furnishers!!!... Then, the great decision:
Choosing a lodging – Okay: Speak with the concierge!
We speak with him. At your beck, the monster emerges
From his cave, offering you a slimy basement, or better
A mansard that you don't want for anything. –

Onward driver! elsewhere: from the first to the sixth,
We must see everything. So much the worse! I'll take the third. –
Contradictory, tooth-and-nail debates over the price.
And the parents! One must still know their preference.
They come and see. "What filth! what are you thinking? a lair,
A grotto! How do you expect us to visit you
There below?" A double door is needed,
An immense corridor, and marble within:
A statue or two in wood, or clay, or plaster,
Representing Venus, Mercury, or Cleopatra...
And all the *et cætera*... "Whaddaya think, mama!" –
The mother-in-law assumes the attitude of a *caiman*
To snap at that toad of an inconceivable son-in-law.
We kill ourselves to find a lodging that doesn't exist:
"It's too high! it's too low! it's too near! it's too far."
Then, in chorus: "It's too dear!!..." In the end, one seeks a place
To hang oneself!

          Let's go then! – O cutie,
The land where untrammeled love flutters
Is near to hand: I would like to show you the way,
And to follow the path while giving you my arm.
I would like to dedicate my entire life to you, and even
My portion of paradise or hell, – I love you so much.

But when you say to me: "Let's get married,"
I grow very rigid, seeing before my eyes
That steep path that leads to city hall,
Peopled with fiacres and red tape,
Whence human beings, sweating in their habits, vexed
By their boots, leave in austere carriages.

Well! cutie, let's sleep in each other's arms tonight
Murmuring softly: "What happiness is ours!"

The Last Waltz

Under the divine bow: spin round crazy girls,
Under Olivier Métra's divine bow.
The waltz falls in Niagaras
With its sad flats and joyous trills.

In the middle of the loud *taratantara*,
Relax your torpedo flanks:
The sylph of the ball, the prince of quadrilles,
Will lift you up on his arms of steel.

Strangely warm, strangely pale,
The woman twists under the male's embrace.
Like a crazy circle rising from the parquet.

In an inexpressible and dying vertigo,
The bow is a lively whip that fustigates.
Luminous demons: spin round in the night!

To the Woman with Blue Eyes

Like a feverish person looking for the sleep that eludes him
I went along, silently and gloomily into the night,
Far from everything that sings and shines,

Walking my somber ennui under the somber sky.

The stars seemed extinguished for good,
Dead forever the saintly illusions;
I no longer had God for my empty embraces,
I was wandering, stifling lamentations in my throat.

But you appeared, young radiant star,
Letting, in the gloomy and tumultuous chaos,
A ray descend, pure like a look from the gods.

And my soul, accustomed to black sarcasm,
Was reborn to love, to dreams, to the light.
Greetings to you! Greetings, o first youth!

Sonnet

Oh! your flesh! your white flesh! oh! your all-naked flesh,
The shiver of your undone hair that leaves
And winds like garden snakes from your face
To bite your breasts and fleshy shoulder!

To see you one night again! and in your emotional bosom
To hear the sobs of a profound delirium,
And to feel in your flanks the fits and starts that muscles
Make, and nerves, when drunkenness has come!

Oh! to take your body again, and in its voluptuousness
To forget all that this love has cost me:
My long nights, my feverish days poorly recovered from!

And to kill the desire that follows me everyplace!
For in the very marrow of my bones I feel the obscene hysteria,
And the blood of my heart is a river on fire!

Sonnet

When I repose in the pit finally, tranquil,
Having around me the eternal darkness;
When my members will have lost all movement,
And my empty orbits the look that sparkles;

That being that was me, that poor fragile nothing,
Forgotten, will sleep – bones for eternity–
And, far from the vault of heaven, silently,
Nothing will move anymore under bed of clay.

But you will last forever, eternal beauty,
Outside common death and caducity:
Your body cannot die, being my soul!

Also, one fine evening of love, when over my tomb,
At length, the shadow of that woman passes,
You will wake, skeleton lover of Beauty!

Sonnet

I have many times wept all alone, in my hovel,
Far from you, far from you whom alone I loved in the world,
Far from your charming kiss and far from your blond love,
Like an ugly demon expelled from paradise.

I repressed the disdained sobs of the accursed.
And, when revelers hailed me to join the round dance,
Crying: "Come with us! drunkenness washes over us!"
In its casket, my heart chanted a *De Profundis*.

And when I followed them into their celebrations,
On my lips, all ready with intense laughter,
Was concealed the glacial rictus of the moribund.

You who could never see the love in a soul,

You who could never give as much as you take,
What does it serve me to implore your hard pity, o woman?

The Other Side of the Model

I

By dint of seeing in Gothic temples
Madonnas in their mystical capuchins,
Beautiful and smiling at their worshipers:
The very seductive Saint Johns or old Josephs;
By dint of seeing blond sinneresses
Letting their thick hair flow like waves,
And their naked breasts stand up like flowers, –
Shameless and sacred privilege of sorrows! –
By dint of seeing under enormous porches
Venuses spreading their immutable shapes,
And bronze nymphs in their proud nudities,
And surprising sphinxes sculpted in marble;
By dint of seeing, in countless museums,
Queens with their foreheads banded with iridescent pearls,
Princesses dreaming while leaning on a balcony,
Marchionesses with an abbot for a dragon,
Impure women, and myriads and myriads,
Hotter than loathsome nightmares get,
I wanted, – o dreamer! – to touch that ideal
With my hand, and to find in that lineal fold
A palpable form, the which, full of life,
Could appease my ever inappeasable flesh,
And to take you with my lion claws,
O Galatea, as Pygmalion did.

I did it. –
        I found the impeccable model,
The woman escaping the tableau conceived for her;
And I loved her in my imagination
With a heart previously skeptical to every passion,

But as the wind of the dream warmed with its breath; –
And I believed I held my ideal! O what an oaf I was!

That myth has brought many together, under the cypresses!

    II

One evening as she was dreaming with eyes open, near
The large hearth where sparks cascaded,
I wanted to see behind her pupils,
And I went, like a heroic seeker,
Through the open pupil, into the heart
Of the belle whose glory a hundred tableaux sing.
I saw nothing at first, so dark was the pit!
Then my eyes adjusted to that obscurity,
And I sounded the other side of my dear beauty.
Alas! In the somber hole where my avid gaze
Plunged, I found here, there, nothing but emptiness;
The taciturnity of impure sepulchers;
And when I wanted to write my name on the walls
Of that cenotaph with indelible ink,
The walls were nothing but dust and sand.

An atelier, at night! The forgotten brushes,
And the dry palette with its blended tones,
Very empty tin tubes, half open,
Grey torsos, modeled arms, inert things!

Yet, she was dreaming. – The perfect model,
For the *line* demanded that she should dream like that. –
But behind the canvas there is no woman,
Art being unable to capture a person's soul.

She was dreaming! – "I'm hungry," she said rising.
And I was even sadder than before,
Sad and upset to have, like a naughty child,
Broken my precious toy to understand the mechanism.

The Fall

The beloved and perverse gipsy
Deserted her Middle East
With their expansive, luxuriant landscapes
To go into lucrative business.

In a cabaret she pours
Liquors for students;
Me, on my knees, a supplicant,
Brutal despair rocks me.

Now, we are four or five of us there
Around that girl of zinc,
Whose cold astuteness plays on us.

But Samson courts Delilah!
My dream fell into the mud,
And I followed it there.

Song for Nini

Tuesday, day of rain.

Fly away, dreams of a day!
Spleen under the downpour drowns us...
Who gave us nights of joy?
    It was love.
When I said goodbye to you, my brunette,
Do you know, Gipsy with the bronze-colored breasts,
Who separated us?
    It is fate.

I wrapped my two arms around
Your young and supple waist,
And I believed my force invincible;
    It was love.

Nothing remains for me now,
Except to cry alone, all alone,
Over my happiness wrapped in a shroud:
    It is fate.

I remember the contour,
Childlike and pure, of your cheek,
And your mouth that pouted:
    It was love.
In the importunate solitude
The wind whistles a mocking tune,
And I hear my heart break:
    It is fate.

At the hour when pleasure hastens,
I feel you palpitate and alive:
Your life is the wine that gets me drunk:
    It was love.
My tears fall one after the other:
I hear as if a knell of the belfry,
For now you are dead to me:
    It is fate.

A god, said to be deaf and blind,
Bought me in a lot of slaves
For an odalisque with serious eyes:
    It was love.
But, filled with abject rancor,
A goddess, blind too,
Set me free, mercilessly:
    It is fate.

The Beauty and the Beast

You never understood, o wild Gypsy,
What mad passion cast me at your feet,
Roaring like a lion that an acrobat beats;

Your infantile caprice and dark complexion tormented me
With the inept persistence of rage;
And on my vanquished face your conquering foot was placed.

For all my snuggling up in a corner of the cage,
And groveling and acting more despicable than a dog,
You came to revive your wild animal.

You had nothing to fear, and you knew it:
The iron rod gleamed in your small hands,
And I was too dominated to do anything about it.

Also, emboldening you by my sottish cowardice,
You took my heart, and, piece by piece,
You tore it alive with your little teeth.

Alas! these great leonine loves are too beautiful!
You don't understand them, and prefer the more playful
Beasts that one sees running after your decoys.

And me, coward! despite so many inflicted wounds,
I licked the hand that had tortured me,
While you turned your gaze to your conquests.

The jibber-jabbering parrot; the large tiger;
And the bear that dances so the dominatrix laughs, –
All had the very desired kiss of love.

The lion, the menagerie's deposed king,
Roared with the sobs of a slave under your blows;
And the group hissed at that doleful beast.

Let's go then! I have broken the chains and bolts;
Far from your whip, I run to the ideal empire:
You will not see your beast at your knees again.

Oh! don't lure me with false smiles
Into your night traps; don't make me re-enter at all

The love cage, witness to my martyrdom;

Do not make your big animal cry again;
Because he could, one evening, go off the rails,
Rise up and seize you and devour you...

But you don't understand that, o wild Gypsy!

Artistic Revenge

Here is my heart, here is the anvil:
Tap! but tap on it then!

I was born, far from your mists,
In a land of moss-covered oaks.
My father was a friend of dreams,
And in the marble he woke
The souls of Venus and Eves,
Rugged sculptor, by mallet blows.
He dominated the indocile stone;
And, under the hammer, the chisel,
Nimbly, like a bird,
Ran from thin lips
To fingers made spindle-shaped,
Chipping away at her breasts, at her haunches,
And pecking away at her white thighs,
Nimbly, like a bird.
May flowers be brought to my father
In his old abandoned tomb...
For he is dead, his heart wounded!
The dream sometimes makes the artist
Despair, after wearing him down.
One burns in the fire that one kindled.
Old faggots, dashed hopes!

Here is my heart, here is the anvil:
Tap, but tap on it then!

The pure musician, my master,
With his long, tense fingers,
Under the living bow, he made the soul
Of empty violins come alive.
He belted out four chords:
Re sol do fa, do fa re sol,
The group of scales, the hordes
Of *ut* sharp and *si* flat;
And from inanimate things
Drawing out vibrant armies,
With his foot tapping on the ground.
Then, in a strange effervescence,
His eyes glazed over, and he stopped.

God tempted him again!
He is dead from his powerlessness
To render what he felt.
A singing breeze consumes
Many an unperceived springtime.

Here is my heart, here is my anvil:
Tap, but tap on it then!

What does dying matter? And what difference
Does the dismal attempt of old age make?
Better is the strong sensation
That makes our aorta throb
And that shortens our instants!
And what difference do aneurysms make
And hypertrophy and bile,
Provided that, rich in sophisms,
The passion of prisms
Gives us a specter in a rainbow?
Far from serene altitudes
I prefer to mark my weeks
On the calendar of Love,
In a book of profit and loss
To keep a reckoning of my days.

I want to avenge myself on woman
By some sweet epithalamion,
Marrying the marble to the musical scale
And creating, like Memnon,
A statue possessing a soul,
Which, under the light of the sun,
Would forever chant my name!
What does it matter if I burn out and fume,
Under the kisses I received?

Here is my heart, here is the anvil:
Tap, but tap on it then!

Last Day

Take your dress, take your plaits, take your jewelry! –
Go, I have loved you well, and I found your feminine
Gestures of a crazy she-cat exceptionally sweet! –
Take your lips and your eyes, your body wherein, for me,
The ideal horizon of desire is contained. –
Take them, take all these talismans of pleasure away.
– Go, I have loved you well! – Ah! take also, come to think of it,
To store it in your heart, the flower of remembrance!
For these last eight months of prodigious love
Were gay and dashing and tender, weren't they?
– Go, I have loved you well! – Today, it is my door
That opens, and I say to you: "The devil take you!"
Without bitterness, with a slight smile. –
It is the law of the Golden Calf, my dear: things change!

Now, we don't live in a wild landscape:
Let's respect that police officer called "busted."
You must leave us now! Go to the *bal de l'Opera*.
Your young face among the old will shine.
Your beautiful, black eyes will be the new Ursa Major
That sailors of the Stock Market navigate by,
Abdomen and chest cram-full in galleons,

Rolling, pitching, decked out, ballasted with millions,
Making sail with silk blue paper currency
That the Banks of credit swell, wind of joy;
They will drop anchor around your corset;
And one of them will untie the knot of your laces. –
– Go, I have loved you well! – In eight months, what a party
Until you said to me: "I have a huge headache!"
– Don't think of me anymore, never, never, never!
We were poor, – be very rich and very distant, but
To avenge the time when several pink radishes
Made up the menu of our morose meals,
Be terrible, take them for all they're worth,
Let lines of concern fill the forehead
Of the man who pays for the pearls in your crown!
Don't console me, I'm laughing, don't you see, my pretty one!
I know Paris too well to despair;
I know the way things roll in Paris, to well to weep.
Ah! you are quite right: "Love is just a caprice!
And as such, it must entail Vice!"
– Go! I have loved you well these last eight months! – Tonight
Let's laugh again, to chase away boredom with big embraces.

Hold me in your arms, and let my thoughts
Roam over the Ocean of my cradled dreams!
...You don't want to, until tomorrow only?... Ah! poor us!
Take your dress, take your plaits, take your jewelry!

Same Old Song

          I

If I had the wings of an angel
Large wings with blue reflections,
Far from the earth and dirt
I would fly towards heaven;
I would spread them wide
One fine, clear summer evening;

As the spirits of legends,
Silently, I would traverse the air;
In a single bound, I would enter the heavenly abyss
Full of attractive vertigoes,
I would embrace the sublime sky
In the amplitude of my roaming arms,
I would dip into space,
Quite high in the eternal azure,
And onto a cloud that passes
I would climb like Ariel;
For I want to fly to the stars,
And fall asleep in their elements.
O world full of disasters,
Let me run far from love.

II

If I cannot to the stars
Forever guide my flight;
If I cannot like sails
Open wide my golden wings;
On some winter night
Made of fog and disappointment,
I want an infernal force
To open the subterranean abyss for me;
Among the nitrate and sulfur
Of old mysterious volcanoes,
I will throw myself into the chasms,
To disappear from human sight;
For company I will have fountains,
And for friends will-o'-the-wisps;
I will never stop my journey,
From one dark relay to the next,
Until I reach the center, where funereal gnomes
Will bury me far from daylight.
O earth, full of darkness,
Let me run far from love!

Scattered Music

Charm me, celestial music,
Comforter of dark days,
When, thanks to fatal abandon,
In the lonely soul there remains
Only a tomb of old hopes.

Charm me, distant music,
Let the wind carry me;
I love the uncertain harmony,
Of the ungraspable flute,
That haunts the stirring evening.

Charm me, extraordinary music,
That I heard in my heart,
When in my dazzled mind,
The rejoiceful clarinet
Intertwines with the derisive violin.

Charm me, music of masters,
Full of laughter and sobs,
Symphony with wide-open windows
Where traitorous flats and sharps
Ride at infernal gallop.

Charm me, naïve music,
That climbs from the court pavement,
Slow and plaintive romance,
Or poor, sickly lament
That a blindman bawls out to the deaf.

Shreds of the ancient sonata,
Old minuet that forgetfulness chews on,
A disparate grand air of the opera
That an organ drags by the feet,
Cradle my sorrow that falls asleep.

Lost Words

Oh! Those women! Those many women one encounters!
    Those beautiful eyes! Those beautiful, so cold bodies!
Pawn your watch, poor dog, put it in the Mont-de-Piété[16]
    To pay for such obscene octrois.
Oh! the debauchery that puts you under their claws
    Panting from head to heart,
So that you might exit more sullied than their rags,
    And emptier than a columnist!
Oh! to spend an ardent life and youth,
    Youth that is prompt to tarnish,
Unable to stop and without knowing
    How things will finish!
Oh! to place an ideal butterfly on their lips,
    And not feel that they have
For all men, all, except silversmiths,
    An equal and deep disgust!
To forget so many virgin and solitary hearts,
    Steamy chalices of pure love,
And to go and drag to horrible mysteries
    All the dreams of gold or azure.
Gentle like lambs, dreams refuse to go
    And say: We do not want to!
Then they cede, vanquished by folly, and they are used
    In one knows not what dark battles.
Ah! a thousand times better, than those rascally wenches
    That one perches on a pedestal.
Better, a brutal and stupid brothel
    Full of pimps and pallid girls;
At least, when you come down from the aphrodisiac
    And the gloomy bed with its old springs,
Only your cadaver haunted the barracks,
    And your heart stayed on the street.
While if you take one of the free girls
    From the entresol or the sidewalk
You can use all the sinews of your soul,

---

[16]*Mont-de-Piété* – a chain of pawn shops popular in France at the time.

>   Priest of a hopeless cult.
> Some say: I will never love but a few, that's a caprice,
>   The killing caprice of moments;
> Then one goes back again and again, and one slips
>   Into sensual embarrassments;
> Hallucination take you like a vertigo;
>   One turns, one descends, one loses oneself;
> Passion deliciously fustigates
>   The sots it casts into hell.
> In the world's insouciance and miscreancy
>   Satanism knocks you off;
> One barely awakens to the cries of degeneration
>   That a noble and old instinct let out.
> Always too late! – And one man lodges in his head
>   The ball of a pistol;
> Another man, having prepared his soul for every shame,
>   Lies in the bed he has made for himself.
> And from that dead-for-love and dead-for-shame,
>   Quoted in the stock market of the heart,
> The girl makes a good prospectus which she relates
>   With a mocking smile.

Redivivus

And now, you have seen, my dear friend, enough women
Who offer you pleasure without giving you love, –
Stop turning your songs into stupid epithalamions
          For all those caprices of a day.

Look, if you can, look hard under the cinders
Whether the flame has remained in your heart's hearth,
And whether from the uncorked flask one can take
          One more drop of liquor.

See if all is quite dead in your holy youthfulness,
If your sun has no more warmth or rays,
And if fate wants your soul to be reborn

Under its ancient illusions.

O your illusions! keep them, if any remain!
A naïve dream itself is worth more than a diamond.
Reascend with feverish step that fatal slope
      That leads to disenchantment!

You will say that your heart fell into a mire.
Eh! The rain of heaven also. But, in the first sun,
Look: that muddy water transforms into a cloud,
      And floats in the shiny firmament.

Say goodbye forever to all vulgar love!
The girls of Epicurus make the grave mistake
Of not having a heart at all, and hardly having a brain...
      Look farther, love higher!

Goodbye! Mimi Pinson, Musette, crazy girls,
You in whom I believed as one believes in hell!
If I played my part in your joyous quadrilles,
      Alas! I paid too dearly.

Adieu! Manon Lescaut and Marion Delorme!
Have you laughed enough at my naïvety?
If you want to wait for me, wait for me under the elm:
      I have often waited for you there.

Alone!

I went all alone, vaguely, through the woods.
The grass had shivers, and the trees voices;
The amorous birds sang their melodies!
On the branches, it was the same old comedy
Where, in conformance with ancient denouements,
The nature-poet united his lovers.
Why am I all alone?... In my oppressed soul,
Tenacious, with effort, I followed my thought;

I murmured verses in a small voice, a new plan;
I was the austere lover convinced of beauty;
What do I know? My spirit, prisoner, turned the millstone;
And, seeing my youth thus lost and alone,
Through the bushes the blackbirds whistled at me;
Under the mosses derisive flowers turned the other way;
Looking through the silky blades of grass,
Like a curious child through its fingers,
Together they laughed, not without reason,
At that passing dreamer, alone like a Robinson.[17]
I fled, carrying the drama in my head!
Everywhere the same song, alas! and same celebrations!
At the back of a cabaret, under the green trellis,
A bourgeois wedding party: they were at dessert;
They drank; the good old men sang ancient verses;
The bride, with her poetic veils,
Grew red in the face each time a clever fellow, full of humor,
Said with great emphasis: Love! love!
Further away, in the clearing, a couple, happy and young,
Snuggled up in the grass and did not act niggardly with
The delicate and long kisses, with the sweet coo coos...
And I fled, gloomy pedant, saying: "What sots!"
O springtime! o springtime! amorous nature!
When an adolescent, impious and proud, rips
From the pages of his heart – love, that charming word;
Believe me, in his madness and in his pride, – he lies.
"Ah! Though around me people sing, laugh, love,
I would rather," I told myself, "finish this poem!
Let's see: the handsome Lindor appears, and his rival
Provokes him; Lucinde, alas! faints..." –
And very softly spring was singing its little song:
"Do you recall, poor man, Rosine or Annette?
Their round necks, their stunning breasts,
And their red mouths?" – Oh! be quiet, spring!
And stiff with wisdom, absurd with anger,
I fled far into the woods that springtime illumines;
I went, wanting to curse my leisure, searching
For all that can make a man vicious,

---
[17]like a Robinson: Robinson Crusoe.

To be alone, and to flee woman, his sweet dream,
And to prove himself deaf to the seductions of Eve...
– "Let me work!" I cried, furious;
When I passed, I was frowning.
Poor fool! I was leaving nature – admirable prey...
For jealous and somber art, for shadows.
Now I saw, every which way, arms that intertwined,
Eyes that sought each other out, hands that squeezed:
Young men, slow and gentle in their behavior,
Followed fresh skirts that springtime makes smart-looking,
I was mad! I climbed the one hundred steps, I entered
My mansard and I said: "I will work here!..."
Alas! as I was sitting before the blank page,
I remembered, dreamer, that it was Sunday and
That the year before I had run through the great woods
And that *She* was warbling with her sweet voice,
And that I was filled with joy like other men,
And that all my ideas, all my phantoms,
The glory that I sought, and the applause,
All the noise, and splash, that gratifies for a moment,
And that leaves a terrible emptiness at the bottom of one's soul,
Altogether, is not worth a single woman's kiss.
And looking at the dismal walls like a shroud,
I said to myself bitterly: "Why am I all alone?"

Sonnet

Where are your sweet looks and your white shoulders,
O foolish women that I loved when I was foolish?
You have disappeared, all of you, I don't know where;
And my heart is filled with tombs and willows.

Spleen, son of Calcraft, has hung a rope around the neck
Of my verses, verses that sang formerly, clever and joyous,
With the music of love, employing new expressions...
Adieu, silk dresses; adieu, velours... froufrou!

I took a frightfully severe mistress:
Crampon! you put water in the wine of my glass.
And my sober forebears ought to be satisfied.

I don't dare to inquire whether sour destiny
Intends another mistress for me in the springtime;
But the mistress I thrash today, it is poverty.

THE GREEKS

Queen of Spades

(Dialogue)

SHE

Psst, psst, psst! where are you going, poet Pique-Étoile?
What appalling melancholy veils
Your eyes that I would love to see open like flowers?

POET

A Flower of Bitumen has caused me my sorrows!

SHE

Psst, psst, psst! I am good, and green hope
Peoples with its rays, during the inert night,
The hour when my elect spend time close to me.

POET

Of the iniquitous Golden Calf, I have suffered the bitter law.

SHE

Do you know the secret of smiling veins?
Silver gleams in the half-opened pocket of queens!
Like the gods, here's the jack, then the king:
The glittering aces are taken for stars.

POET

The temple of love collapses on its pilasters.

SHE

Psst, psst, psst! my hallucinating palace is such
That, despite remorse, my reign is immortal!
Submit to me! Say goodnight to your bastards of Eve.

POET

I want to imprison my soul in the dream.

SHE

Psst, psst, psst! I have the key to the avaricious treasure,
Where all that one can conceive of for the price of gold
Becomes reality in the shape of a dream.

POET

The desire of an impossible power gnaws at me.

SHE

Psst, psst, psst! come! keep your disdain for others.
I am the ancient and grave girl of Destiny:
My army of Jacks guard the Imaginary!

POET

Would I touch with my finger the face of the chimera!

SHE

Psst, psst, psst! I know marvelous philters,
That chase away hunger, thirst, and sleep in the eyes;
My lovers' arms have no lassitude.

POET

Let's go, I am yours, wild and rude Queen!

The Greeks

One evening Æmilius, the prince of rotten luck,
Resolved to win – *Mataia*, vain thing –
Some talents with one of his Napoleons
In an obscure gambling den, not far from the Pantheon.
Night fell: Phoebe showed her timid face;
The player donned his woolen chlamys,
And to the den, where Ploutos presided over combats,
He sauntered, like the steers of Ajax, his feet in stockings.
The Greek temple opened its hideous postern
At the end of a corridor, true path to Avernus,
Where Phoebus-Apollo was represented
By a spent lantern in the acidic obscurity.
Æmilius entered under the plaster vault;
And suddenly an ephebe in a yellowish apron,
Who responded: "Vlaboum!" when one interrogates him,
Welcomed him on the sill. The crowd that was yelling
Stopped, contemplating the young proselyte;
But, as he did not have the look of a satellite,
The pensive Achaeans went back to their game.
A thick smoke filled the holy place with its stink.
Seated on tripods of austere craftsmanship,
The players held in their mouths a crater,[18]
And their lips emitted, by powerful expulsions,
Clouds of incense directed toward gaseous suns.

The ephebe was seen here and there in various groups:
On the marble tables he set down his his cups,
Glass amphora with solemn heads of foam,
Where yellow and white nectar frothed, hydromel
Which Gambrinus,[19] Dionysus' old rival,

---

[18]crater: synecdoche for a cigar, when the lit end has a concave shape.

[19]Gabrinus: the mythical "patron saint" of beer, brewing, and all that goes with it.

Brews with hops and authentic barley.
On a zinc altar a thick-lipped Greek was enthroned,
Sticky like an old Priapus; but also stocky,
To whom, for this reason, all Diogenes' sons
Showed more respect than to the twelve gods of Athens.

Meanwhile, in the crowd, a cry rang out:
"Name of Zeus!" – Some big shot, having laid an egg, clucked:
"Cut! Cut! banker!" (*To cut!* verb of prey
Whose future optative: *I am going to win*, is employed
With the verbal *nine*, or the diminutive *eight;*
And to *do Charlemagne* is an infinitive,
Whose present punters[20] will be participles...
Confer Nieburh, *passim*, Burnouf: First principles)
The punter Æmilius, pale, trembling, captivated,
Listens to that noise like a siren's song.

Several Thessalians with their stinking cnemides,
Subtle Argians, draped in their clamydes,
Bent over men, come out of Sion, Cretes
Escaping their native soil, above the straits,
Athletes who have no fear of the gods,
Daughters of Lesbos, women of Corinth,
Their trained fingers earning gold deniers
That the Boetians would offer to the god of fate,
And that, laughing quietly, garnered Perfidy.
The bank fleeced them, those pigeons of Arcadia!
Popoï! Æmilius didn't look at them;
He saw only the winners of combats,
And sought, – poor fool! – for the gold in his belt.
That nebulous temple, that impure atmosphere...
Everything excites him!... It is gold dancing joyously in his eyes!
The encephalon bursts into flame with a simple rubbing
Of your wheel, o Fortune!... Let's go! here's the prey!
Æmilius standing, approaches, and, full of joy,
Throws onto the baize a metal coin.
Adieu, dear silver sheep: here comes the butcher's block!

---

[20]punter: a gambler, particularly one who bets against the bookmaker.

THE GREEKS

O degenerate Greeks! O sons of Themistocles!
If your bronze forebears descended from their pedestals,
And, leaving for a day the Champs-Élyséens,
Came to contemplate you, pale Athenians;
Those who spilt their blood in Scamander's[21] waves,
Those who carried Alexander's glory far and wide,
Pheu! Pheu! what would they say if they saw their sacred name,
Their name which is the pride of the Parthenon's walls,
Which keeps the summits of Mt. Taygetus still standing
And the indigenous cohort of gods still in memory,
Their name to cover like a nasty copper blade
The brazen theft of the sweaty knights?
On finding that ambiguous aspect in the Greek word,
Socrates would willingly drink his cup of hemlock again,
Old Demosthenes would spit out his pebbles,
And the prolix Isocrates would fall silent before you!
O dead of Marathon! soldiers of Salamis!
Marmorean heroes that ancient glory shines on!
It is with écarté[22] (from the Greek word *écartaïos*)
That your counterfeiters fleeced Æmilius.

Æmilius lost every last copper coin of his.

Poor Boetian whom fury makes drunk!
The Achaeans laughed! Æmilius sat down,
And, noticing his cup untouched, he grabbed it,
And, highly strung, smashed the vessel on the ground.
Then, to pay for the damage, he left his petasus;
And casting an intense look at the Greek temple,
His heart full, he exited completely broke.
The player felt sick to the encranion;
He cursed under his breath his stupid escapade:
"I swear," he said, "by the subterranean gods,
I would like to hug you and break your back,
O Greeks!!!..." He addressed himself to the greedy Argians;

---

[21]Scamander: the ancient name of the river Menderes, in modern-day Turkey; it flows into the Aegean Sea.

[22]écarté: a two-handed card game.

Too late! his hands patted his large, empty pockets:
Adieu, fields where Ilion once stood!
And he shook a fist at the walls of the Pantheon,
While Scythians,[23] by order of the archons,
Came, at a measured pace, to arrest the punters.

---

[23]Original footnote: The archers who were charged with the responsibility of keeping the peace in Athens were also called "Scythians."

A SEASON OF SPLEEN

I Would Like to Live in the Woods

I hate you, o cities! vast sepulchers of stone!
Expanses of wall! ocean of roofs! dark horizon!
When at sunrise he open his eyes,
A man feels surrounded by the horror of prison.
Rise, birds, into the air where your wings beat.
Here below are hard hearts and tight masks,
Noise, whirlwinds, fog and mud.
      I would like to live in the woods!

My mouth is filled with bitter irony;
Over my face a shroud of spleen has fallen;
My dream of the Ideal, Love, or Virtue,
Disappears far from me, fugitive chimera;
When my illusions, sweet unfaithful woodpigeons,
Have no more voice to sing on the deserted doorstep,
And escape into the sky with the loud sound of wings...
      I would like to live in the woods!

To the rhythm of her breasts, pure masterworks of orfevrerie,
My mistress cradles my body in her arms,
At the hour when a kiss is planted on her lips,
Like a joyous butterfly that never grows tired.
Then nothing: the charm evaporates, the idol lies soulless;
Adieu, forgotten pact of amorous rules!
The temple reverts to a thatched cottage, and the angel, a woman...
      I would like to live in the woods.

Let's debate!... One went to sit down: young men,
Beardless but pensive, who influence potentates;
Politics, in the imbecilic times that we live in,
Is a worm in the tomb that gnaws at the Estates.

Me, I'm tired of the back and forth of words
By those iconoclasts, those regicides;
And farce or tragedy, alas! those are the roles we play...
       I would like to live in the woods!

Oh! in your cabarets filled with the songs of the crowd,
When absurd melancholy, which I enjoy,
Descends on my eyes, and when my soul is drunk
With the society that makes men ugly,
I grow anxious to forget gaslight and smoke:
In the mirror that provides an escape through your narrow walls,
I evoke quietly the beloved perspective
       Of the path I lost in the woods.

Round of Remorse

I exited a bitter and stupefying orgy
Where my reason had burned like a vine shoot;
Heavier than lead, the ambient atmosphere
Made my twisted bones crack with deep despondency.
The fever shook the partition of my temples,
And in the white and red circle of the lamp
The horror of visions rotated cruelly.

Feminine perfumes mixed in the room
With the troubling aroma of cigar smoke:
Vague scents of iris, ylang-ylang, and amber,
And some grains of seraglio formerly burned.
My ears rang with memories of the orgy,
And the steel hammer of cephalgia
Sprouted in my brain nameless dreams.

My flesh was bruised, my soul so tired,
And my heart so anguished for spleen,
That I fell into an armchair, near the mirror,
To see myself again like a long-lost friend.
And I looked at myself for an hour like that.

The mirror made my image so pallid,
That I looked like a ghost scared to death.

Suddenly, a terrible voice inside me
Made my nerves jump, and leaving my closed mouth,
Despite myself, it filled my abode
With a lugubrious cry, and I felt afraid without knowing why.
With a metallic ring, the voice said this:
"Here are your beggars! here your dead! here your clique!
Accursed man! look at the remorse that walks before you!"

In the mirror they marched past, one after the other,
All bad and shady acts, with lowered head,
Chewing obscene paternosters with their teeth;
And their procession went forward step by step.
Behind them, secret calculations, villainies
That you performed, o my heart, and that you vainly deny,
Like hunchback midgets waving their arms.

Others, amidst the noise and hullabaloo,
Drunk, and dressed like morticians,
Carried coffins full of murdered illusions
Whose souls and bodies I'll never see again.
What defunct dreams of heroism or glory!
What cadavers of love soiled by black mire
Have been trod underfoot by those specters of Remorse!

Then all hunchback midgets and all the dirty beggars,
With the atrocious and dismal joy of Evil,
Made their rounds around those debris,
Whom an infernal orchestra invisibly guided.
And in the whirlwind I don't know who leads me:
Hurrah! it's Saint-Guy, the obscene tarantella,
And I dance the Bacchanal ballet with them.

Dark night, when I see so many cloistered disgraces
Coming out of the past to offer me their nudity;
When the torrent hurls over its locks
The mire of my heart and its iniquity...

Alas! when the sun, tapping on my window,
Woke me, I understood that, last night maybe,
The river that I had drunk from was not Lethe.

The Long March

I set it too far, too high, my life's dream,
Beloved future vision, pursued
      Over long days of mourning.
I had left home, joyous, without looking back:
Alas! I put faith in my warrior strength,
      And I had nothing but pride.

For a long time, I counted the road's milestones,
And said: By walking in this way, clearly,
      I will arrive there by evening.
And each step followed the other, from valleys to hills;
My dreams were distant, and my stars lofty;
      And the blue sky turned black.

A mocking *trompe l'oeil* foreshortened the distance,
The object grew larger, but the goal assumed the exorbitance
      Of a shadow that would come at you;
The steeple stood out strongly against the moon:
Another step, and still that wood and that dune!
      Walk rather on your knees!

It would seem to be the last kilometer.
And, feeling his desire and his strength renewed,
      The traveler does not stop at all;
And, when he has walked another several leagues,
In the prolongation of blue perspectives,
      His end is even farther away.

To desire! To become! That is the law of nature!
To march ever and always! March! If, peradventure,
      You touched the goal with your hand,

Leaving behind you the oasis and the source,
Towards another horizon you would pick up your course:
    You must die on a path.

Desperando

Tomorrow, tomorrow! That terrible word, filled with charm,
That to your walls, o old Paris, led me,
Makes many a tear fall in the shadows clearly,
And raises to heaven the cries of the damned.
That is what egged me on, that is what said to me: "Climb!"
And what said: "Be strong, be hard, be pitiless!"
And so that hope alone might guide you, go, shamelessly,
Crush Love and Friendship underfoot.

O Paris! vortex of passersby who go quickly,
Thrown like sand to the four winds;
Disheveled crowd where all is precipitated,
River of Oblivion that runs to death, to the sea!
In that immense crater where your swell stirs,
From Montrouge to Montmartre, from Auteuil to Bercy,
Among that unknown, indifferent crowd, nobody
Is concerned about the stranger that arrives.

And there I lived, without concern, without distress,
Under the blue sky always with a golden sun;
I had frank, joyous friends and my mistress,
And the breeze of the sea at the hour I went to bed.
And I wanted to leave! The seductive mirage
That made fairy Ambition sparkle in my eyes
Cast me into a gulf and made a castaway of me; –
And the wave will be your winding sheet, Halcyon!

Misery's Gibbet

O God, whoever you are, Destiny, Mother Nature,
Why did you draw me out of the shadow of Nothingness?
Respond! why did you create your humble creature
Only to crush him under your hard, giant heel?
Who could force you, impassive Eternal,
To nail me to the human wall, like a target
        Destined for the arrows of Evil?
Weren't you rich enough in teeth to chew?
And was it necessary that my jaws should join
        With you to chew in infernal concert?

Oh! The dreams I have at night; I must have committed a crime
In some ancient world, and I am damned!
But you may go back to sleep, Executioner! – On your victim
From head to heel your fist is unrelenting.
Vainly, I open my arms, like a bird spreading its wing,
        To repatriate with the skies;
You have nailed me too tightly to the wall, eternal
        And harsh vengeance of the gods!

I am like a thief on the cross, lowering his head
Under the bleeding hair that dangles. Formerly,
I lifted up a face that mocked the tempest
So as to blaspheme with a strident voice:
Satan had given me a formidable laugh
That shook my sonorous nerves; despite you,
        Delirium came to intoxicate me.
Today, it is over: you have vanquished me, clearly;
My head, dropping to my chest again, hears
        My heart, filled with tears, weeping.

There was a time! On that vile path, I saw
Several men passing, happy, thrice blessed;
In the evening air the perfume of a woman wafted,
And the birds made their nests on my gibbet.
I am alone! the passersby no longer pass! The earth,

Distant, as far as the horizon, is a widow and solitary;
    The birds are dead, I am alone!
Thin, tortured victim, without a dream and without a fatherland,
I see my withered youth day by day leaving me...
    Misery is a hard shroud!

Imprecation

If ever I acquire the power,
I will go straight into their lairs;
Like a specter of vengeance,
I will make them white with fear;

Under the exhalation of my anger,
Their Arrogance will disappear;
Like the arch of a stone bridge,
Their back will bend under my fist.

I will hear from their mouths
The prayers and the sobs,
And in the ferocious silence,
My face will be impenetrable;

I will tear their spine
With the scourge of my disdain;
I will consummate their ruin,
And sit on their remains.

My irritated face will glow
With a strange gleam of joy,
To see stretched out in the mire
Those who jeered at my poverty.

Toward the Tombs

I would like to be underground
In a well-sealed chamber
And there, in the solitary night,
Find those who loved me.

I would have many things to say
To those poor, cherished beings,
I would bring them roses
And geraniums in bloom.

And their souls, in those dwellings,
Would respire that dear perfume,
And I would speak of defunct Time
For hours on end.

How is it that I remain
On this earth with the living,
Where Evil comes like the plague
On the wing of thirty-two winds.

There, I am alone, like an islet,
Without friends, hearth, or gods;
There, I drag a sobbing heart
Amongst hateful mockers.

Where are my cherished hopes,
And my dear illusions?
Where are the ephemeral Dreams
Peopled by stars and beams of light?

They have died, they are underground,
In my friends' tombs;
There, in mystery's den
Where their ghosts sleep.

O dead, leave your cheerless beds,

Come back, terrible and silent,
To see me sometimes in the darkness:
If not, I will go find you.

Mortal Triangle

You make me suffer, o cruel woman,
You make me cry the cries of the damned,
And in the torments of the present hour,
To curse the cold and sensual love,
And false happiness, that you give me.

You make me suffer, morose ambition,
Which furnishes my heart with disappointed dreams;
Your smile lies and your voice fawns:
You have let me fall into the ditch that lines
The barely-perceived fields of Triumph.

You make me suffer, voracious poverty,
Enticing spleen, a demon that is happy
To strike men fallen in the scum,
Even though a dandy of haughty race,
A lord like Byron, a king like Hamlet.

Oh! triply formidable enemy: Woman!
Present troubles, future Dreams,
The vile viper's venomous skull,
Fiery triangle that enters my soul,
Trinity of Evil, you kill me!

?

Isn't it right, Mephistopheles, that with laughing and weeping
Humanity conjugates a single verb: To ignore?
One can comb the earth, bore to its center,

To discover what embryos it holds in its belly;
One can swing through moving Space,
Hear the Wind's voice, read the Cloud's face,
Aim for the stars with one's regards, –
The Sphinx has no Œdipus at all: it sits impassive
On the sill of those parched and lugubrious deserts
That Religions populate with their debris.

How surprising is it then when a vanquished man decides,
One night of horrible anguish, to kill himself?

Dilemma

If I want to endure intolerable Indigence
Openly, nobly, dark Destiny pushes me down;
And if, letting my heart pursue its desire,
I cull a flower of Pleasure under my eyes,
Dark Destiny crushes me even more and says: "Coward!
Return to your hovel and return to your task,
Die in the harness, be the poorly noticed slave
Of hopeless labor and Poverty!"

To that I could respond as any other might;
And, weary of the obscene dungheap I wallow in,
Take four pieces of coal, behind closed doors,
And pray to Nothingness to stifle my sobs...
 * * *
 * * *

True Triplets of Misery

    I

THE WIND

Why do you weep? asked the Wind,

The winter Wind loaded with plaints.
Your situation is very moving then?
Why do you weep, asked the Wind,
Are you the only living being
Who could sing such complaints?
Why do you weep? asked the Wind,
The winter Wind loaded with plaints.

ME

I responded to the winter Wind:
Others are joyous: I suffer;
This existence is a hell!
I responded to the winter Wind:
Spleen, that bitter comrade,
Leads me with large strides toward a gulf!
I responded to the winter Wind:
Others are joyous: I suffer!

THE WIND

Ignore the violins,
And the amorous refrains.
Paris has many other distractions.
Ignore the violins;
One sees, from sidewalk to downspouts,
Ruder sorrow than yours.
Ignore the violins,
And the amorous refrains.

THE WIND

Listen to what I tell you
In a minor scale, very sad.
Do you hear the voice of the damned?
Listen to what I tell you.
You will think yourself in Paradise
In that artist's cellule.
Listen to what I tell you,

In a minor scale, very sad.

Voices Carried by the Wind

II

A FAMISHED MAN

I haven't eaten since Sunday,
And it's Tuesday, almost midnight.
Here's the butcher! God! What a slice!
I haven't eaten since Sunday!
I smell the white dough rising!
The baker groans, and the bread bakes.
I haven't eaten since Sunday,
And it's Tuesday, almost midnight!...

A HOSPITAL NUMBER

I writhe at night on my hard bed,
And I bite my fists to avoid crying;
How to assuage fierce pain?
I writhe at night on my hard bed.
But I keep quiet! If I opened my mouth,
They would come again to torment me.
I write at night on my hard bed,
And I bite my fists to avoid crying...

A TRAGIC, SHORT-SIGHTED FOOL

Thunder of fate! It rains buckets!
If I had what it took to sleep a bit...
A rocking, warm bed is so good!
Thunder of fate! It rains buckets!
Under this deserted bridge I cross,
The Seine attracts me with its blue sheet...
Thunder of fate! it rains buckets!
There, I will have what it takes to sleep a bit...

THE NEGLECTED WIFE

I will light the coal,
And close the window.
The merchant said it's good.
I will light the coal.
What's he doing, my vagabond?
With another woman perhaps...
I will light the coal,
And close the window...

A SUSPICIOUS PASSERBY

The first that passes, I'll need to speak with him:
Your money or your life! After all, one is a man!
I begged; someone said to me: You make me laugh!
The first that passes, I'll need to speak with him...
Oh! midnight! The wee one'll have nothing to fry;
I must steal or we all die of famine!
The first that passes, I'll need to speak with him:
Your money or your life!... After all, one is a man!

THE BANKRUPT

Tomorrow morning, it's bankruptcy,
With dishonor in the end.
My daughter sleeps, poor little one!
Tomorrow morning, it's bankruptcy!
Me! In this accursed fix
I will drink my last cup...
Tomorrow morning, it's bankruptcy
With dishonor in the end...

THE CONDEMNED

Hey! who calls me there? – Would that be the hangman? –
No: – it's the shadow of death that pursues me in a dream.
To me it looks like it's nailed to the windowpane. –

Hey! who calls me there? – Would that be the hangman? –
To say that they will place me in their black tumbrel,
After having split me in two, like one splits a bean!
God! who calls me still? – Would that be the hangman?
No! it's the shadow of death that pursues me in a dream.

III

THE WIND

What do you say,
Eh! beautiful mask?
Battered heart,
What do you say?
Your virtue
Is quite flaccid.
What do you say,
Eh! beautiful mask?

Hope!

        * * *

Eh! weary of the obscene dungheap I wallow in,
Less patient than Job, I could, like any other,
Take four chunks of coal, behind closed doors,
And pray that Nothingness stifles my sobs.

But no, despite fate and bitter Irony,
I hear the distant flight of the young chimera:
"You will be king," the smiling specter says to me,
"You will be like a prince of the Orient,
You will be glorious, and on all heads
Your foot will step the proud step of conquerors.
Sleep now! Your sadness will sleep, your sorrow
Will vanish tomorrow; gaiety will blossom
Once again; woman is nought but a dream,

A dream that a sigh of your soul rouses;
It appears great and beautiful, but when your will
Blows on it, it's nothing in reality."

"What does beauty matter, what does a statue matter?
It will be brought down by the hand of time.
And others will come along, child,
To people the triumphant's heart with their loves,
To interlace your face and your crown with their arms,
And to say: 'What I have of love, I give it to you.'
What has fled from you will be dead, like a
Fine cloud that will swell the common gutter;
Others, a hundred times more beautiful and loving,
Will burden that soul with mute torments.
Go vanquish! For as you know, the volatile hearts
Of women are the ardent prey of vanquishers."

"What does your absurd poverty matter, and the tenacious
Obsession of the cold usurer who menaces you?
Imagination makes your future grander:
A sky filled with long, never-ending palaces,
With marvelous festoons, astragals,
With Heliogabaluses' diamonds,
Inebriated boudoirs of modern perfumes,
Circuses and baths worthy of bygone ages,
And sofas, and chandeliers, and antiques,
And the eternal sun casting light on porticoes...
Sleep, child, and dream of the splendid future!"

And I blew out the bitter lamp, to fall asleep.

Promenade

When night covers the earth,
I go through the solitary woods
Far from the noise and mocking laughter,
The silence is thick under the oaks,

Everything dies down, both the cries and the hatreds,
And I hear the song of my heart.

All is beautiful in the unfathomable night,
O my eyes, towards the formidable azure
Lift up! Sadness sleeps!
The horizon grows obscure in the silence:
Ariel takes off to the stars,
Illuminating all the golden lamps.

O my soul! be attentive!
Hear the captivating music
That escapes through the forest:
It is the old and new song of Zephyrus,
A languid murmur that sighs
As if nature wept.

It's the voice of the hills and valleys,
It's the harmony of lofty stars,
That make me, full of dreams, dream.
One respires an infinite love,
It's your sap, o blessed nature!
And I want to plunge deeper into it.

And I go through the solitary wood,
When night covers the earth,
Far from the noise and mocking laughter.
The silence is thick under the oaks,
Everything dies down, both the cries and the hatreds,
And I hear the song of my heart.

Awakening

That nightmare! How long did it last?
I don't know: three months? six months? – Is it true then
That I called you, o death, or destructrice,
In the inexpressible and wild caprice

Of a spoiled child wanting to take the moon in its teeth,
And immediately see what's inside?

There it is, in that small room where I work,
Where the sun, piercing the open window,
Makes the dust dance in swirls, and causes
The good old laugh that cheers me.

O dear sun of May, which makes us live and laugh,
Which chases away old spleen, chases away the vampire,
Greetings! The mortal nightmare has lasted too long.
That's fine! let the horse of night, at a gallop,
Escaping from bright Phoebus with spread wing,
Carry it off forever, faraway from my eyes!

In the Old Fashioned Way

Suffering! you are just a word, a vain word! I defy you!
Let fever pour all its poisons into my breast;
Let laughing seasons be erased from my days;
And let light be stolen from my sunken eyes.

Let friendship for me entail only betrayals,
Let gossips blather my withered name,
Let yesterday's freedman, a slave, the son of a slave,
Fill exile and prisons with senators!

Let me be damned by Destiny, the coward,
And let a lictor tomorrow strike me with his fasces!
What do I care about this appalling life and death?

I have followed the advice of Stoic sages;
Draped in my pride like an ancient hero,
I can be broken, but I will not bend!

On the Way to Charenton[24]

Strange burial!
An angel
Is nailed into a coffin.
Four heavy bizarre
Guitars
Trundling along, lead the bereavement.

In an acrid smoke
Formed
By the lover's pipes,
The shadow of the treacherous
Mistress
Advances tranquilly.

Farther away, a very old
Bottle,
From which cognac was drunk,
On the slippery pavement,
Traces
Of steps *ab hoc ab hac*.

A surly phantom,
Flat-out broke,
Beneath a squashed hat
Opening its enormous mouth,
Inquires:
"Who of his are dead?"

The diabolical spleen
Replies:
"It's a frail *mirliton*,
The soul of a very nice
Poet,
Carried off to Charenton."

---

[24] Charenton: a hospital for the mentally ill.

The saucy bottle
Rattles on:
"I softened his brain."
"Oh!" said the little female
Skeleton,
"My flanks were his cave."

The guitars, lame
Singers,
Grating with despair
Whine: "Poetry,
Paralyzed,
Is a lugubrious buzzkill."

Now, my vile, soulless
Carcass,
Leaving the sewers,
Looked with a stupid expression at
My head
Going to the land of fools.

Since then, through the servile
City
And among the open fields
As if in a foreign land,
I wander alone,
For no reason, shouting songs.

Don Quixote

When they had had their fill laughing at señor Don Quixote,
That obstinate pursuer of the giant Ideal,
They went to bring their offerings to Baal
And became pure slaves to the stock market.

Without a care in the world: no slap, no kick,
They showed everyone the trivial project

Of making a bestial banquet out of life,
And amassed gold, hand over fist, in the dung.

The poet walked on like an old fool, lifting
His disheveled head to hear the wind,
While they divvied up gems and large sums of money.

Now, the poet was hungry and thirsty; but they laughed at him.
Then, as they tread on his heart and mind,
He cried out: "Don Quixote is dead, long live Prud'homme!"

Being in Paris

(A Song)

When the old blacksmith's hammer, Destiny,
Flattens me on the anvil like a penny's worth of butter,
And brushes aside my lackluster future,
        My soul bleeds and weeps;
        But, being in Paris,
        Jocular town,
    From morning to evening, I laugh if off,
        And laugh, laugh.

When that horrible evil, a poverty in hat
And clothes, once black, that wearing takes the bloom off of,
Gives me a dark and cold nimbus of discredit,
        My pride bleeds and weeps;
        But, being in Paris,
        Jocular town,
    Like Diogenes, I laugh it off,
        And laugh, laugh.

When on the green baize, peopled with dreams of gold,
The ace of clubs, that triumphant god, deceives at me,
And when rotten luck reduces my savings to nothing,
        My wallet bleeds and weeps;

        But, being in Paris,
        Jocular town,
With a sallow laugh, I laugh it off,
        And laugh, laugh.

When woman, that sweet synonym of *ennuis*,
That source of life that God wants to die for,
Turns my day into night, and vice-versa,
        My love bleeds and weeps;
        But, being in Paris,
        Jocular town,
Like Mephistopheles, I laugh it off,
        And laugh, laugh.

When the Ideal on a soap bubble,
Having launched me toward the capital,
Blows, and when I go where the bubbles go,
        My dream bleeds and weeps;
        But, being in Paris,
        Jocular town,
Like a Philistine, I laugh it off,
        And laugh, laugh.

I am not the only one to act like a ham
Who lies and changes his mind every hour:
Drama in the *coulisse*, and farce in broad daylight,
        Jean who laughs, and Jean who weeps;
        But I am in Paris,
        Jocular town,
And when I weep, I laugh,
        And laugh, laugh.

Bitch of Poverty

On feeling myself hounded by that filthy beast
In the street, where people see me pass,
I hasten my heavy step, I'm so ashamed, and I'm

Constrained to lower my head.

Why don't you leave me alone, o bitch of poverty?
When will you stop barking at my heels, and when,
O scrofulous rabid cur, fierce like an ulcer,
    Will you buzz off?

If I'm sleeping, I hear you ululating in my dreams,
Companion! and on a bad night I see you;
And, as soon as morning rises over the blue rooftops,
    You wake me with your barks.

Why howl like that? Your baroque hurlings
Attract the tailor who demands his goods;
When, after long days, your fangs have shredded
    The suit that wasn't mine.

Your cries attract everyone; the glum laundress,
The lugubrious cook of a greasy spoon, the exasperated landlord,
And even the man clothed in blue wearing the *tricorne*[25]
    Who, annoyed, makes me beat it.

It's raining! Like a thief I must run out
In this downpour, half diving, half swimming:
Bitch, you have lost my last umbrella,
    And gobbled up all my money.

I never attempt an errand, nor a trip,
Unless it's by walking on my two tired feet,
For you have often had my passage refused
    By conductors of omnibuses.

Tonight, leave, o vile, o preposterous beast!
Long live the dear flasks that make life enjoyable!
I am drunk!... But what! there you are again!
    It's fine, as one must pay.

Your chronic barking woke up my mistress:

---

[25] man clothed in blue...: in other words, a policeman.

Alas! she's flown the coop, sweet put-out bird,
For the Golden Calf, that ideal boor who is caressed,
    And never barked at.

At last, I'm at my wit's end: I wish you were dead,
Unable any longer to endure your suffocating company.
For the last time, see that door...
    It's time for you to beat it.

HISSED!!

A Tragi-Comedy in One Act

Renown

RENOWN

Hey! Street poet,
Look how the people rush forward
To hear my hurlings!
I'm afraid my stage will buckle!
The hands and feet of the crowd
Are full with applause.

THE POET

I like the voice that sounds and the bugle of glory,
And the noise of drums, whether in fairgrounds,
    Or in the graveyard.

RENOWN

Behold the winners of the race!
For them the crown and purse,
And blessed hallelujahs.
Hey! respect my theater;
Don't be boorish like a shepherd:
Leave your loves in their nests.

THE POET

Loves, flown away towards a romantic sky,
Have caused me too much suffering to begin anew.
    My old dreams have hardened!

RENOWN

Contemplate the laurel of masters!
At evening, close your windows
In order to work all night.
Desire the harvest of palms!
You must keep your passions calm,
To have days full of noise.

THE POET

I know that ancient heroes and geniuses
Aimed, after death, for infinite spheres.
       One wants everything immediately today.

RENOWN

Hey! Oh! the footlights are on;
The large cash register is an anvil
To forge celebrity on.
Poet, roll up your sleeves,
Sell us your heart in slices
From a licensed publisher.

THE POET

What do suffering, sobs, bitterness matter,
When Glory appears to cut through the fog?
       The applause has tempted me.

RENOWN

Eh! Hey! The fight! The fight!!
Don't go playing the flute
At the bank of Paris streams!
Pick up tempestuous trombones!
It's to the loudest on the trumpet
That I'll award the prize!

THE POET

Glorious lie! When one lifts the curtain,
Harlequin is a monarch and Colombine a star.
        Poor dream, I've been cheated!

RENOWN

Curtains! that the public might see
Your sadness or your joy!
You belong to the public.
Kiss, disdain, caress, or slap,
Let them applaud or hiss you,
Be my obedient serfs!

THE POET

That's right, o Renown, immense poseur,
Flip our hearts over with the toe of your boot
        On the resounding stage boards.

Hissed!!

The scene represents a park. A wooden bench at the foot of an oak tree. In the distance, a path, a villa.

ROBERT

He enters, looks around to be sure that he is alone, throws his hat and his jacket on the grass, then pulls a watch out of his fob.

A quarter to five!... I don't have long to live.

He sits down and stretches a rope out on his knees.

Like a heady wine, suicide intoxicates...
One evening, one grows tired of fighting, of chasing
After the illusion that vanishes. – Better to die!...
Then one backs off, better to banish that idea...
Get back! – Never weary, it keeps you glum.

Everywhere the tempter!... It's a river, at night;
The pistol that eyes you, the dagger that gleams;
At every street corner a rope;
Every tree on the path you walk down accosts you,
And says: "See my branches: they're strong and tense.
You can cull emptiness here, if you like!"
Poison for the rich, a river for the poor,
More than a thousand roads lead to the graveyard...
One must be treated like a king down there,
For no one has ever come back...
Basta! – My death will put a nice end to the week.
Now, let us summarize:

He takes a notebook from his pocket and reads.

                        Tuesday, calm day,
General rehearsal; – very good! –
Played Wednesday evening, and... hissed! – Thursday... nothing.
Friday, read the journals: pitiless criticism,
Panned! – What an incredible bludgeoning!
Poor illusions! not one remains standing!
I staked everything I had on that cursed drama!
Nothing – not even honor – remains: Defeat!
Rout!! Waterloo!!! I hear, in my head,
The sound of their booing. – Let's go on: Saturday,
Put my accounts in order calmly 'til midday!
Wrote my testament! – My net estate,
My property, all said and done, parbleu! my debts.
Also, so my uncle might remember me,
By autographed epistle, and papers providing proof,
I have chosen said uncle for legatee!
He disinherited me, him! before the notary...
Me! noble heart, driven by good intentions.
I made an ingrate my inheritor.
What an effect that posthumous letter will have!...
But as for that letter!...

He reflects.

HISSED!! 87

                      Oh! as usual,
My natural absent-mindedness made me take a wrong step:
I receive a letter, and I don't read it...

    He pats himself down, looking for something.

Sad!... At one point I placed it on the top of my desk...
Then exited... Who sent me that epistle?

    He looks through his pockets.

Nothing.

    He rises, rope in hand.

           Would it be you, uncle with the severe expressions,
Uncle with a heart of granite, lawless and unbridled uncle,
Who shoots a Parthian arrow at your nephew Robert
Before he departs this world for on high?
With maledictions perhaps, grumpy uncle!
With envenomed prose and upsetting words!
But what am I saying? O nephew, whose wisdom is small,
The hell if your uncle, from his distant province,
Thinks of someone else than his friend the coffer!
Him, write to you? Come on!... To tell the truth, I'm wrong
To be looking for that unfindable letter. – What difference does
The emptiness in life make, when one finally opens the door
That gives on that black landing, Eternity?

    He stands up on the bench and throws the rope over a branch.

Good rope!... Perfect! Combines solidity
With good taste; fifteen sous! That's small potatoes.

    He gets back down.

                                          On the moss
Let's leave this note.

    He places a piece of paper on the bench.

                    Sad and sweet offering,
Last thought and last breath;
And the last dream of a fool who is about to die!
– And that's what happens when you love great ladies!
One wishes to become rich and famous; one writes dramas...
And one hangs himself! – What a pathological, drunk, and crazy god
That Lord Cupidon is! He leads, one knows not where:
Me! a poet – or at least an attempter at rhymes –
I love, I adore to the point of committing crimes...
A banker's widow; yes, that's where I've gotten myself to!
I can explain: she's Italian,... and then,
Those feet! those hands! those eyes! that smile
And the morbidezza that cannot be described...
A widow at heart!... Heart that no one can touch!
Oh! I've tried.

He walks up and down anxiously.

And here it is six months later, after I met her.
What verses, what sonnets! God! what a basketful
Of poems she has received!

He stops dead in his tracks.

                    What did she say?
She must have mocked me, no bones about it.
And to think that I'm on her property, at several meters
From her villa! – From here I can see her windows...
I'll go find her, tell her everything?... But...
She'll have me thrown out of doors by her lackeys!...
Then, timidity, that demon that obsesses me,
That contorts me, or that makes me freeze,
Would paralyze me before that beauty
Whom I dare to love... from afar. – Oh! the timidity!!!
It would be better...

He climbs back up on the bench; then he turns toward the villa..

            O my divine one, at the hour when dawn sings,

When you exit tomorrow, pensive and nonchalant,
To breathe in the morning air, what a fright you will have,
Seeing there, blue, in his tight halter,
A young man, well-attired, hanging from this foliage,
Like an old signboard for a village inn?
Spectacle assuredly devoid of any gaiety!
Perhaps you might say: That's sad, in truth!...
Especially when you find out where so many rhymes came from,
Burning madrigals, anonymous sonnets...

He interrupts himself.

Patati! patata! I'm babbling on, things
That make no sense, and the time is running short.
Oh! for all that, I had a heroic strength
To compose those Latin discourses, in rhetoric!

He starts humming, while preparing a slip knot. During this time Bellina appears; she does not see Robert, and is not seen by him.

BELLINA *has a fan in one hand and a bouquet of flowers in the other.*

The time is ripe; the sky is clear like a mirror,
And all the wood quivers in the evening.

She tosses away her bouquet.

BELLINA

The scent is a little too troubling: it intoxicates me...
One could say that on this sweet spring evening life is good!
But I'm bored! Drats! I've received nothing
In eight days from my crazy anonymous rhymester.

ROBERT

He has passed the robe about his neck, and prepares to kick the bench over.

One kick with the foot, and I'll leave this world for another.

So be it! May God have profound pity on my soul!

BELLINA

Noticing him, she hurries and prevents the bench from falling over.

Sir! what are you doing?

ROBERT

        Madame, I'm hanging myself.

BELLINA

Go hang yourself elsewhere.

ROBERT

 In an aside.

       Ah! the happy ambush!
Not upset to see me a captive.

BELLINA

 In an aside.

       And nobody around!

 To Robert.

Get down then!

ROBERT

     Will that please you?

BELLINA

          I order you.

ROBERT

> *With a keen attitude.*

If I hang myself, I ought to have some reason for it.

BELLINA

And me, I'm here at home, on my property.

ROBERT

But I too am the proprietor of my life,
And I can throw it away like a cigar butt to the ground,
When it's not worth anything anymore.

BELLINA

                                            Understood. That's up to you;
But get down, for God's sake, or I will call out. – A hanged man!

ROBERT

That brings good luck: you can keep the rope.

BELLINA

Will you get down?

ROBERT

                    Before I consent, madame,
To what you ask of me, by heaven swear to me
To give me enough time to tell you why
I am sad... and gay, full of love... and full of hatred,
So as to suspend myself from this oak branch.

BELLINA

Distancing herself.

But he's mad! Whoever he is!

She calls out.

John! John!

ROBERT

In a lively manner.

Ah! for pity's sake,
As somber destiny gives me this opportunity
To be able to recount my story, deign to hear me out.

BELLINA

With dignity.

Would that be a wager?

ROBERT

Taking up the rope again.

Eh, fine! I'll hang myself.
There, seriously, if you take another step,
If you call out for John, whom I do not know
And have no desire to make acquaintance with, the hell
If that obscure henchman finds at the other end of this rope
Anything else than a deadman when he arrives here.

BELLINA

In an aside.

And there is nobody!... good God! how foolish I am also
To be walking about all alone!

ROBERT

                                    Oh! I will die soon enough.
I suffocate easily, having had bronchitis.

BELLINA

    In an aside.

Damn! Looks like he'll do as he says; but wait!
I cannot let him hang himself in front of me!

ROBERT

    Politely.

While it pleases you to listen to me, madame,
To elucidate to you the thing, I require
From you the time it takes to say four *Ave Maria*.
For what it's worth, my parents raised me quite well.
I will not say anything that cannot be heard.
On these conditions, I consent to come down
From on high where I hover between you and the sky...
By comparison, the sky gets the short end of the stick.

BELLINA

    In an aside.

Looks like I'll have to give in. It's all rather titillating!
After all, he does not have a nasty face.

    To Robert.

Go on! Speak, monsieur.

ROBERT

    Descending.

But no tricks!

BELLINA

Ah! From where you stand, tact... and reason,
Spirit, and good manners... I'm terribly afraid, I swear to you.
A hanged man!!

ROBERT

   I am neither traitorous, nor foresworn,
And I did not come to pillage or to burn,
Nor, as my rope here attests, to speak
To your grace...

BELLINA

Interrupting him.

   But what then?...

ROBERT

       To leave existence behind me,
And to see how it feels at the top of a gallows.

BELLINA

Suicide! my God!

Robert, in a dramatic tone of voice.

ROBERT

   Unrelenting suicide!
When one says: Better it is not to have been born at all!

BELLINA

Interrogating.

And you are, monsieur...?

ROBERT

> *Bowing.*

> > Robert.

BELLINA

> *Interrogating.*

> > Robert... of?...

ROBERT

> *Simply.*

> > > Carcassonne.

BELLINA

> *Laughing.*

Excellent nobility!

ROBERT

> > We harm no one!
And that is what sets the Roberts apart from everyone else.
The Roberts of Cantal, the Roberts of Gers,
And Robert the Devil, and Robert-Macaire,
And Sir Robert Peel, English minister,
To whom one owes free trade.

BELLINA

> > In all honesty,
Monsieur... de Carcassonne, such gay warmth,

On the subject of death, is a noble thing!
I suspect, however, on that score, something else.
Aren't you a little too quick to fly off the handle?
Are you not a bit too... gay?... too?... too?... not to mince words.
You wouldn't happen to be crazy?

ROBERT

                                      Of course not, I'm a poet.

BELLINA

It shows.

    In an aside.

        A poet! oh! oh!

    To Robert.

                                    I'm listening.

ROBERT

    In an aside.

My verve and my boldness seem to have left me...
O timidity! be gone!

BELLINA

    Seeing that he does not say a word.

You wanted to say something...

    She sits down on the bench, and offers him a place.

Monsieur...

    Robert sits down at the opposite end at first, then draws near.

Oh! but farther away!... That's better! I'm listening.

ROBERT

Madame...

BELLINA

Eh, well! Is that it?

ROBERT

To tell you the truth, it's hard for me
To make my introduction, and I'm confused.
Wouldn't it be better if I were hanging up there
Than to be sitting down here a Pierrot, mouth agape,
Making you languish in scant proper fashion?
But I really cannot figure where best to begin.

BELLINA

Eh, well! I will be good and confess you.

ROBERT

In an aside.

She's divine! Let's go, my friend, buck up!

Humbly.

Confiteor.

BELLINA

Let's hear it then – what was so serious
As to bring you to this, you, light-hearted poet,
And so foolish that death even cannot turn
Your smile into tears, your springtime into snow?
There must be a plausible reason, a... what do I know?

Unless you just love strangulation.
After all, that could be a vocation.

ROBERT

No, certainly not; but death beckons me.

BELLINA

                        Ah!, really!

ROBERT

    With some emphasis.

I plunged the scalpel into my soul,
Weighed the pros, weighed the cons, argued
Against myself, for myself, and commented on
Phædo[26]... in Greek; and I had, I confess,
Such contempt for the world, for its luxury, for its filth,
That I would not leave behind me
A trace of a regret.

BELLINA

             What did humankind
Do to be able to merit such profound hatred?...
This poor humankind!...

ROBERT

             What has the world done for me?

BELLINA

Well, yes!

ROBERT

---

[26]Phædo: a dialog on the subject of the soul by Plato.

What has it done, to me particularly?

BELLINA

Certainly.

ROBERT

It hissed me!

BELLINA

Hissed?

ROBERT

Categorically.

BELLINA

Fancy that! it's true... a poet!

ROBERT

Explaining.

A volume; Lalune was
The publisher; price: three francs.

He gets up.

O sinister fortune!
I had some success among the refined sort;
But as the vulgar didn't think much of it,
I wanted to surprise them, strike them with the blow of a master...
That's where destiny was waiting for me, that old traitor!!

He sits back down.

So, here's my story in a few words: I had
Eighty thousand francs worth of property, I could have
Drawn much profit therefrom, planted carrots and cabbage,
Planted vine stock and collected bundles
Of hay, I would have raised cows, I would have made
The milk collaborate with old platras,
I would have repeated the deluge for my wine,
Like any other man, I would have employed subterfuge;
In brief! I would have made it rich, and I would even have been
Mayor of my commune and later a deputy.
But... my father died, God forfend! My head
Seemed to me to contain the brain of a poet,
I heard novels jibber-jabbering in my chest!
There I was then, off for Paris, with a conqueror's step.
Having taken possession of my small patrimony,
Transmuted my oats into gold coin,
In any case, I was going to eat my inheritance.
Poetry, alas! didn't produce anything for me!
Then, one evening, nearly out of money, but not courage,
Like a Benedictine I dedicated myself to my work,
And I gave brith to a drama... Oh! don't be afraid,
Madame! Happily, I don't have it on me.
Finally I was produced... and hissed: a total failure!
A cyclone, a whirlwind, a *strong* tempest,
Have never equalled the vocal power
Of fourteen hundred keys that hiss at the same time;
Something that moans, that meows, that lows...
It's extraordinary, madame! A sound to make the deaf-mute
Blind; At the top of their lungs, they made echoes,
And wakened with horror the shadow of Jericho!

BELLINA

That's really terrible!

ROBERT

            So, leaving my drama behind,
I departed, shamefaced, with death in my soul.

Such a debut is a devastation:
My purse is without a dime now and my life has no purpose;
When one has fallen so low and so deep,
To climb back up a little, madame, one will have to hang himself.

> *He climbs back up on the bench.*
>
> *In an aside.*

Well and good. Oh! The stupid idea!

BELLINA

> *In an aside.*

He will not hang himself...
A false Gascon hanged man!

ROBERT

> *In an aside.*

And there's my problem;
I don't know what to tell her.

> *He looks like he's about to place the rope around his neck.*

BELLINA

Eh! there,... monsieur!

ROBERT

Madame?

BELLINA

I'm sorry to disturb you in this way, but...

ROBERT

My plan

Was this: five o'clock, hanged... the rope awaits me.

BELLINA

                                                     Eh well!
Let it wait, I want to renew the conversation;
I want, do you understand?

ROBERT

                      An order! splendid,
I will inscribe it in my notebook: Delay, an act of God.

BELLINA

Inscribe it then. Speaking of which, do you know the lesson?

ROBERT

What lesson?

BELLINA

                My God... you're rather thick!

ROBERT

    In a lively manner.

Ah! behold the great word of bourgeois wisdom!
When between two old bankers, shamelessly rambling on
About things of art, and if one of them says:
"So and so died of hunger yesterday evening... without question
What's done is done... he wanted to be the bird that sings...
Couldn't he have just played cards and gambled to pay the rent?"
It's a botch job. It's quite nice to laugh a little at fools
Who seek something above the filthy lucre.
Eh well! me...

BELLINA

                But, sir, come down...

ROBERT

He comes down.

                              Me, whom a dream
Has pushed, pursued, persecuted relentlessly,
To then throw myself off to the side of the road;
Me, who will not see tomorrow's dawn,
After having placed my melancholic foot
In the dark circles of poetic hell,
After having worn down my heart, mind, faith,
Love, illusion... until finally the rope! me...

BELLINA

Yes, you?

ROBERT

    Me, I declare them inept, without contest,
All the bankers in this world!

BELLINA

                Let's go, right!

ROBERT

                                Yes, I attest
That Alaric, Attila, the Hurons, the Sioux,
While killing and scalping are three hundred times kinder
Than those men of the stock market, crushing a poet.

BELLINA

Doubtless, their pride is completely stupid.
But... Molière?

ROBERT

> Molière?

BELLINA

> Isn't he also a bourgeois?
A philistine? a vile investor? an Iroquis?

ROBERT

> *Very conciliatory.*

My God, no.

BELLINA

> And nevertheless he covered in shame
Cottin's muse and Oronte's sonnet.

ROBERT

> *Melancholically.*

Molière was right: he was the best.
Does that make the somber judgement of fate less harsh
That attributes to Trissotin a vain love of glory,
Puts between his fingers the quill, and lets that
Ambitious fellow believe that, in his inkwell,
The laurel crowns will suddenly germinate?
And, sad, leaning into the crowd, he hears
The sharp and mocking sound of the passerby's hisses...
And in his revery he returns home shaking.
He has been shamelessly mocked, and Molière
Has cast at that fool all his bile...
He died for it, and nobody complains about it here;
But if one still laughs, if one is not moved...

Me, one of his nephews, I lament and weep,
And I pour out my pity on his dark abode.

BELLINA

Original start! go on.

ROBERT

      By heaven!
Can people be responsible for the bad turns of a cruel fate?
Did it consult with us?

BELLINA

      No, clearly not.

ROBERT

        I'm enraged
To see how one piles it on, by the shovelsful, the outrage,
The hateful sarcasm that destroys, that gnaws at
Those vanquished by art, poorly looked after by death;
Their ridicule has been immortalized,
And their shame will never set,
Nor rest! Against them the world has risen up...
Why? What crime did they commit? Alas! they dreamed!

BELLINA

Bravo!

ROBERT

  Me, I feel sorry for them, those countless unknown,
For whom destiny created days of shadow,
Holding them in lugubrious night and without sleep,
Those who turned their faces towards the sun star.

BELLINA

Bravo! bravo!! bravo!!!

ROBERT

          Far from the well-trodden paths,
After having launched themselves through the blue into the clouds,
When one has passed the Alps and the Himalayas,
Places where absurd prose has never barked,
When one has rubbed elbows with the condor gone astray...
When one has broken his wings, like Icarus,
When one has fallen back to earth from that aerial world,
Not knowing any longer how to get along, good for nothing
When it comes to doing things on the flat surface
Of this petty world... what should one do?

BELLINA

Become a lawyer.

ROBERT

   Surprised.

      A lawyer?

BELLINA

          You speak
Like a book; presto, you are going, you are going...
Trust me: Leave behind you all the poetic hotchpotch,
For to be one of the elect in the political sky,
To speak, but say nothing, it is a certification.

ROBERT

   Horribly saddened by that perspective.

Better is it to be hanged, madame, than to be a lawyer.

BELLINA

Ah! God! You annoy me finally, and... I cannot take it! –
Can one imagine a flatter reason
To abandon life?... a poet hissed!
Fine business that! a stupid dream disappeared!
As if, each time an illusion vanishes,
One should lock himself up in the grave forever.
I pity you. I would never have believed,
I still do not believe in the incongruous plan
To hang yourself from that tree with such ease.
Without a second thought; and that, monsieur,
In my presence!... Stop causing me a nervous fit...

ROBERT

Madame... my apologies...

BELLINA

                    For some poor verse,
To let out that lugubrious cry, that bitter lament!

ROBERT

One feels what one feels.

BELLINA

                    Do you have a mother?

ROBERT

No.

BELLINA

A sister?

ROBERT

No.

BELLINA

But... a circle of friends?

ROBERT

The author struck by the crowd is allowed
To enjoy friendship? No.

BELLINA

Lowering her voice.

How about... a mistress?
Somewhere, far from everything and everyone, a sweet caress
That calms your troubles? Are you not loved?

ROBERT

I receive the affection of no animate being; no,
Not even of a dog.

BELLINA

Who notices the letter left on the bench, in an aside.

His hand writing itself!
It's him! poor fellow! I will find out if he truly loves me!

ROBERT

In an aside.

She does not respond. (*repeating*) No, not even of a dog.

BELLINA

> *As if awakened.*

Ah! yes, of a dog! It's true: you have nothing at all
That loves you! But you?

ROBERT

                                  Me?

BELLINA

                               Do you dream
Only of dramas and have no concern for the daughters of Eve?

ROBERT

Maybe.

BELLINA

    Look at you!

ROBERT

> *In an aside.*

                     Here we go! now is the moment.
(*Loudly.*) Yes, madame, my heart is full of exhilaration.

BELLINA

Good.

ROBERT

> *Hesitating.*

> I love...

BELLINA

> You love?

ROBERT

> A woman...

BELLINA

> A woman?

ROBERT

More and more intimidated.

Adorable... who... whose...

BELLINA

Laughing.

> Oh! my God! what range!

ROBERT

Troubled.

An angel of beauty... (*in an aside.*) Rogue! will you speak? She laughs. That's it! To hell with the impromptu!

BELLINA

Eh good!

ROBERT

> I love her, but...

BELLINA

> But what?

ROBERT

> *Furious.*
>
> But she's dead.

BELLINA

Alas! – Look then for some strong passion,
A powerful thing, a lever, a spring,
Which hardens you against the blows of fate.
For those who really want it, there are noble causes,
Where one performs, without speaking, grandiose acts:
Poetry exists also in combat.
One may be killed, but one does not go hang himself!

ROBERT

What you say is gold, madame, and I would like to believe it;
But to be a hero, even an obscure one, and without glory,
To fall as a martyr, one needs... the opportunity.

BELLINA

Seek and you shall find! I draw a conclusion:
If one comes back empty-handed, worn-out, consumptive...
One stops chasing after the extraordinary;
One follows the broad road and walks forever.
You must turn around and go back. From poet
You will become a banker. Once done,
Believe me when I say it, you won't regret it.
You will look up: the flowers are beneath you.
Why then prefer illusions, dreams, to reality?
Why put sap, force, energy, and winning power,

All, all in your head, and none of it in your heart?...

ROBERT

Eh, by heaven! my heart on the contrary is overflowing!

BELLINA

With what?

ROBERT

    The desire to live.

BELLINA

          That rope
Could prove otherwise.

ROBERT

     O God! this is infernal!
(*Loudly.*) The world is blasé, too contemptuous, too banal
For...

BELLINA

  Banality can be romantic.
And that ought to be with poetic brio
That your heart rises and soars sometimes
Towards your lost parents, even if they were bourgeois.

ROBERT

  Dreaming.

Yes, you are right, I remember: the room
Was quite large and as it was December
We had made a large fire. I was just a child;

My mother, whose limpid voice rang out through the air,
Like a distant song on a silver-string harp,
Made me recite my prayers in Latin;
My grandmother with her white hair dozed near the fire...
I still see her face vacillating a little...
Then, my father arrived suddenly: great celebration!
The dog of the house barked its head off...
My father took me, with a gentle laugh,
And made me jump, joyful, on his knees...
That there is my best poetic dream!

BELLINA

And have you never had the fantasy
Of creating for yourself a happiness like that happiness?

ROBERT

Often; but to do it honorably, one must
Be at least a couple.

BELLINA

                    Excellent! One must have patience.
And be ready for every experience,
In the proud heart one keeps a loving corner;
While waiting, one has himself a romance,
An idyll the color of lilacs and roses...
And as for myself... I will tell you something,
And you will keep it, I think, a secret.

ROBERT

Oh! madame, a hanged man cannot be indiscreet.

BELLINA

Eh well! I have my naïve romance, me, daughter and wife,
And... banker's widow, whose boring routine,

Whose unique preoccupation is, each day,
To speak with Peter and Paul about manure, labor,
Seedbeds, rain and frost, and to discuss firmly
With a sharecropper the yield of a farm;
To be my own steward, and to keep my eyes open
In order to balance the books.

ROBERT

Busy life!

BELLINA

     Oh! yes... valuations and banks,
The three percent, the four and a half... nothing missing.
The actions of the North, the Orléans, the canals,
The biennial and quinquennial foreign loans,
The mines, the Suez Canal, and the Transatlantic,
And rumors of the stock-market! and politics!...
Agents of exchange!... and men of law,
Lawyers, attorneys, turning everything to their advantage...!
Trials... oh! the trials!... speeches for the defense,...
Orders, judgments!... My head hurts...
And I so hate such environments
That I regret being a widow...

ROBERT

My God!

BELLINA

Interrupting him.

An occupied life!... With so many important affairs,
Each day I have barely four or five hours
For my toilette....

ROBERT

Finding that number quite sufficient.

You don't say...

BELLINA

Clarifying.

       And my visits! But,
Despite all those troubles that never end,
I have conserved my right for adventure, for dreaming...
No banal intrigue, oh! no; I am on strike...
Declarations, I know them all by heart;
The coquettish air, the stylish, somber and vanquishing air,
All the airs, nothing new, that Lovelace sings
Make me laugh, nothing but an ugly grimace,
That makes one cry, but makes me happy:
A whiff of smoke! a nothing! that vanishes
At the flutter of a fan... I have better: a mania.

ROBERT

In an aside.

I'm being raked over the coals!

BELLINA

With some irony, and looking at Robert.

       I returned from Italy
Eight days ago; one evening, I returned; I received
A letter, a love letter, my faith! Verses composed
Rather well for the form; and basically very lyrical,
A bit crazy, but with a melancholic tone,
Amorous and suave like a bird's song...
Those rhymes caught me up in a subtle net,
And carried me, on their wings, far from the earth...
I don't really know why, but I let myself go...

One has moments. – Returned finally
From that faraway bluishness were the Seraphim reside,
I desired the expression of adventure...
I turned the page over... Nothing, no signature...
The thing gets complicated. After having dreamt,
Very little, on it, I thought I discovered:
One of my suitors was the author of the poem...
And there I was looking for the most foolish, the most pallid,
To be a poet... Oh! I didn't find what I was looking for.
All starchy, all flushed, the effects of a good meal!
I forgot my Latin, which wasn't hard for me;
Now, as sleep was at my beck and call,
That no dream came to disturb, in forgetfulness
That incident was going to remain buried;
But, after some days, a new dispatch, a new
Modulation on that air: "You are beautiful,
Madame, and I adore you." Then I looked closely:
The handwriting? Unknown; and my memories? Nothing.
Days passed, and the verses arrived by the dozens!
Strophes! sonnets! My hands were full of them.
I found all that very amusing, and I liked it...
An unknown lover was Petrarching me!
I was his Laura... muse and only goddess...
But it threatened to become chronic,
I needed to think: I thought in spite of myself...
For a long time... I realized, one day, not without emotion,
That the unknown man had taken possession
Of my thoughts... And me who used only to laugh!...
Would I love him? of course not! I await without great desire
The lines from his hand, but it is my pleasure
To imagine him, through my thoughts,
Handsome, noble, and generous... It's crazy...
Do you understand any of that? (*Looking at him fixedly.*)
                              He could be, as well,
Some frightening barefoot, bold, good-for-nothing,
Who haunts dives, swears, and drinks beer,
A street poet, accustomed to the gutter,
With long hair falling over his rags,
A caterpillar that cannot metamorphose into a butterfly...

ROBERT

> *With warmth.*

Oh! Madame, that's nothing but a calumny.

BELLINA

Bah! Do you know him?

ROBERT

Certainly not; but I deny...

BELLINA

Oh! oh! look at me, monsieur.

ROBERT

With all my heart.

BELLINA

No, not like that! I am a confessor.
Let me get to the bottom of this completely.
So you know the unknown man? my poet?

ROBERT

Maybe a little.

BELLINA

A lot?

ROBERT

Enough.

BELLINA

                        What's he like?
Personality wise.

ROBERT

        Very sad,... and very gay.

BELLINA

                            That's subtle...
Physically?

ROBERT

        Neither good nor bad in his person.

BELLINA

From where?

ROBERT

                Madame, he's from Carcassonne.

BELLINA

Like you?

ROBERT

        Like me.

BELLINA

    Feigning surprise.

                It's a gross betrayal
And all that has no rhyme or reason...

And me who spoke to you frankly... I'm leaving...
Besides, I didn't say anything, I had nothing to tell.

ROBERT

I agree, but please...

BELLINA

                Again?

ROBERT

Taking the letter off the bench.

                        Read this.
You will see...

BELLINA

        I have no desire to read anything.

ROBERT

                            Thus,
To the last, fortune is cruel!
Booed by the public, and rejected by this lady,
Sad fruits of my waking state, o poor verse, go!
You have no chance!

BELLINA

                Eh! my God! give me them!
   She reads.

    I

*Hear me: this was my dream,
Dream of a child, dream of a fool,
Obstinate, no end, no truce,
That led me... I don't know where.*

II

I saw, one serene night,
A star, a pearl of the skies,
And it was like a Siren,
Speaking softly to my eyes.

III

I wanted to fly to her,
Poor ill-advised Icarus;
The storm destroyed my wings,
And I fell to earth broken.

IV

My dream is not a whiff of smoke;
I've lost my life on earth...
Adieu! you whom I loved so much!
I'm going whence no one returns.

BELLINA

> *In an aside.*

What now?... Now he has hope...
What would one say? At least, we keep up appearances:
That's the most important thing... Great God! if he heard me!

> *Drawing near Robert.*

I saved the life of a fool who was hanging himself.
Oh! don't make me repent this, I beg you.

ROBERT

Madame!

BELLINA

All that is nothing but a pleasantry!
And you love me too little to die so gaily!

ROBERT

Skepticism and gaiety, the outside appearances of the moment!
But that is merely a mask. Today one is ashamed,
When a true sentiment of the heart rises to one's lips,
And leaves it completely freely without disfiguring it,
And the lips smile when the heart is about to cry.
As one lives, so one dies: it's all a lie!
Me whom a cruel trouble gnaws at for six months,
I'm afraid to appear to you impertinent and a sot;
And yet, I have need to tell you a single word:
I love you forever with an uncommon love.
To you my life and my... (*Catching himself.*) I was going to say: fortune.

BELLINA

Poor fellow!

ROBERT

Sorry! I forgot until now
That in my manuscript I swore an oath
To kill myself, that my drama has fallen back down to earth;
That I am ruined; that the solitary hart
Melancholically hangs itself from that green branch,
Awaiting the act, and that I have my place setting
This evening, down below, at Pluto's. (*In an aside.*) What shame!
Ah! vicious scatterbrain! I'm going to settle your affairs!

Someone rings at the villa.

BELLINA

In an aside.

That puts an end to all this awkwardness!
(*To Robert.*) I see you're reasonable now: give me your arm.

ROBERT

No, madame.

BELLINA

      Come again? You have, I suppose,
Forgotten your morose project for good?
You promise, yes?... And... if I have any right
To your thanks, on the day I receive visitors,
Thursdays, you would come, and that will be proof enough
That you no longer think of that new rope.

ROBERT

I no longer think about it; but – I will not come
To spoil this sweet romance. I will take myself faraway,
Without looking back, far into the country,
To live, miles from nowhere, a private life.
In this way, you will keep a little memory of me;
At least, I will not stay here to spoil it.

BELLINA

   In an aside.

Perhaps he is right.

ROBERT

      I also have a ridiculous
Hateful vice, that makes one bow his head in shame and shrink,
A vice that banishes me from the abode of the happy.
I must heal myself before I can be loved.

BELLINA

And what is that?

ROBERT

                Poverty. Poor without hyperbole!
Poorer than Job... not a cent to speak of.

He turns his pockets inside out, a letter falls to the ground without him noticing it.

As you can see: I have good reason to depart.

He bids her Adieu; Makes to leave...

BELLINA

                                            Wait!...

This paper.

ROBERT

What paper?... Well, well!... do you mind?
I hadn't read it this morning... (*He reads.*) What an affair!...
Read! (*He hands her the letter.*)
       My uncle is dead! I'm a millionaire.

BELLINA

What does it say?

ROBERT

                The dear man! He had forgotten to
Disinherit me! Uncle duly wrapped up
Tight in a shroud, sleep in peace! My soul
Will no longer lament you nor blame you!
Be well! (*Bowing.*)
                Madame... at your service: I am
All ready to offer you my arm.

BELLINA

> *Recoiling.*

Monsieur...

ROBERT

I can
Come on Thursdays, and I will make it easily
Four Thursdays and more in the same week.

BELLINA

But, monsieur!...

ROBERT

I will return to my lost dream:
I am no longer hissed! I am no longer a hanged man!
I am no longer collared by importunate poverty!
And I place at your feet my life and my fortune.

BELLINA

> *Ironically.*

Monsieur! Go hang yourself, go. The rope awaits you.

ROBERT

Why mock me thus? You had said however
That you loved the unknown man a little, the poet!

BELLINA

In a dream.

ROBERT

It's a total catastrophe then!
And what do I care for this unfortunate treasure?
What will I do with it, Lord! with all that gold?
I couldn't care less about it. It's you, and you alone I love.

BELLINA

Bah! You can resolve that problem at your leisure.

ROBERT

But set a time limit... not too long, however.

BELLINA

Eh well! we will speak about this in six months.

Robert walks to the tree and detaches the rope.

What are you doing?

ROBERT

The rope... and that heaven might hear me!...
The rope of a hanged man brings good luck.

BELLINA

I doubt it.

ROBERT

I believe it; and the future will not deceive me.

BELLINA

We will certainly see.

Someone rings.

Let's go! Give me your arm.

Exeunt.

Other Books by the Publisher

Fanchette's Pretty Little Foot
by Restif de La Bretonne,
translated by Richard Robinson

Je M'Accuse...
by Léon Bloy,
translated by Richard Robinson

My Hospitals & My Prisons
by Paul Verlaine,
translated by Richard Robinson

Salvation Through the Jews
by Léon Bloy,
translated by Richard Robinson

Words of a Demolitions Contractor
by Léon Bloy,
translated by Richard Robinson

Cellulely
by Paul Verlaine,
translated by Richard Robinson

Ecclesiastical Laurels
by Jacques Rochette de la Morlière,
translated by Richard Robinson

www.ingramcontent.com/pod-product-compliance
Lightning Source LLC
LaVergne TN
LVHW041640060526
838200LV00040B/1649